WILD LION OF THE SEA

WILD LION OF THE SEA

The Steller Sea Lion
That Refused to Be Tamed

by DON C. REED

Illustrated by Norman Green

Sierra Club Books | Little, Brown and Company
SAN FRANCISCO | BOSTON·TORONTO·LONDON

This book is dedicated to the wildness in animals and the animal within us all. As Ernest Thompson Seton once said, "We and the beasts are kin."

The Sierra Club, founded in 1892 by John Muir, has devoted itself to the study and protection of the earth's scenic and ecological resources — mountains, wetlands, woodlands, wild shores and rivers, deserts and plains. The publishing program of the Sierra Club offers books to the public as a nonprofit educational service in the hope that they may enlarge the public's understanding of the Club's basic concerns. The Sierra Club has some sixty chapters in the United States and in Canada. For information about how you may participate in its programs to preserve wilderness and the quality of life, please address inquiries to Sierra Club, 730 Polk Street, San Francisco, CA 94109.

First Edition

Library of Congress Cataloging-in-Publication

Reed, Don C.
  Wild lion of the sea : the Steller sea lion that refused to be tamed / by Don C. Reed ; illustrated by Norman Green. — 1st ed.
      p. cm.
  Summary: Describes the training of George, a Steller sea lion, who comes to California's Marine World as a pup and eventually grows to be a 2,000-pound giant that becomes too difficult for his trainers to handle.
  ISBN 0-316-73661-9
  1. Sea lions — Training — Juvenile literature. 2. Marine World/Africa USA — Juvenile literature. [1. Sea lions — Training. 2. Marine World/ Africa USA.] I. Green, Norman, 1934– ill. II. Title.
GV1831.S4R44   1992
163.088'8 — dc20   91-23720

Sierra Club Books/Little, Brown children's books are published by Little, Brown and Company (Inc.) in association with Sierra Club Books.
10 9 8 7 6 5 4 3 2 1
HC

Printed in the United States of America

Acknowledgments

First and foremost, I want to offer my heartfelt thanks to Robert Gissiner of Long Marine Lab for his suggestions on resources and reference materials and his comments on the manuscript. I'd also like to acknowledge Victor Scheffer, whose brilliant *Year of the Seal* is a classic; Judith King, whose *Seals of the World* will always be a prime source for accurate scientific information on all pinniped species; Finn Sandegren, whose scientific papers on Stellers are so readable and fascinating that they deserve a wider audience; Roger Gentry, whose writing on Stellers and many other species also combines careful accuracy and readability; and Ron Schusterman, whose writings have inspired many people to study pinnipeds.

I'd also like to acknowledge Kathy Krieger, Thomas Orr, Robert Poulter, Paul Bonnot, G. A. Bartholomew, J. Allen, O. A. Mathisen, R. J. Lopp, Ron Kastellaine, Barton Evermann, Charles Scammon, John Rowley, Kenneth Pitcher, Donald Galkins, A. G. Edie, C. H. Ficus, Fred Bruemmer, Robert Jennings, Vinson Brown, Farley Mowatt, Carolyn and Jack West, R. M. Kickley, Frank Stuart, Burney Le Boeuf, Delphine Haley, Marty Snyderman, Jacques and Jean Michel Cousteau, Sally Carrighar, Stephen de Blois, Ron Chaney, Edwin Starks, G. D. Hanna, and the many others whose work has contributed to our understanding of seals and sea lions.

Very special thanks go to my Marine World Africa USA family, who helped me as always — with Sonny Allen, Patrick "Bucko" Turley, Ed Comer, Jenny Montague, Harold Francis, Dennis Hada, and a host of other trainers, animal handlers, and friends helping to fill in the blanks on George's and Eleanor's lives with us.

I'd also like to acknowledge editors Cynthia Bix and Helen Sweetland and publishers Sierra Club Books and Little, Brown and Company for helping my work to see light.

Finally, I'd like to thank my family — Jeannie, Desirée, and Roman — and all my students at Horner Junior High, with a special verbal hug to Period 3, the original and prevailing homework champions.

Contents

A Note to the Reader

This is the story of a giant sea lion named George, a member of the Steller species, who stayed with us at Marine World Africa USA for a number of years.

Everything in this book really happened, but not always in the order in which I've described it. I have jumped back and forth in time freely. Also, I have occasionally attributed the actions of one animal to another of the same species.

Although based on careful scientific research, the chapter on George's life before capture is necessarily fiction, as no human eye was there to see.

With the aforementioned exceptions, this story is true.

It is my hope that this small volume will draw attention to a wonderful species, *Eumetopias jubata*, the Steller sea lion, whose existence in the wild is now threatened.

DON C. REED
Fremont, California
May 1991

WILD LION OF THE SEA

1

First Encounters

Before Nero bit me, I had no particular opinions on the subject of sea lions. In fact, my knowledge of these great seagoing mammals was limited, at best. I knew that at certain times of the year sea lions could be found along the coast of the northern Pacific Ocean. I had once spent hours watching them through binoculars on a rocky California beach. I knew that the males, called bulls, could be fierce fighters. But all they seemed to want to do that day was snooze. They were pretty good at it, too. They lay with eyes shut, barely twitching their whiskers and only occasionally flipping some sand on their broad backs.

I also knew that California sea lions in captivity were often trained to perform in aquarium shows and in movies.

They could be taught to "stand up" on their hind flippers, walk on their "hands," balance balls on their noses, and follow their trainers around on the stage. They seemed shy but good-natured and eager to please.

But there was another side to these marine mammals — a side that I had encountered once, even before I met Nero. My friend Ken Shiels and I were out one afternoon on the waters of northern California's Half Moon Bay. We were trying out a kayak Ken had made. It was a beauty — pointed at both ends, with canvas stretched tight across a cedar wood framework. The whole thing was double-coated with smooth, gray waterproof paint. Ken and I sat in the middle, each holding a double-bladed oar. As we paddled quietly through the low surf and skimmed out across the bay's blue surface, it seemed as if we were heading into the wild. There was no telling what we might find, or what might find us.

Without warning, a bank of gray fog swirled in. It surrounded us and muffled all sound, so that even quiet talk did not seem quite proper. For long moments there was only the chill touch of the fog beading into droplets on our bare arms, and the feel of tiny ripples as we dipped our paddles quietly into the water. Then, suddenly, something huge rose up beside us. At first I couldn't imagine what kind of creature it could be. It was light gold and brown, and longer underwater than our boat. Then a long neck emerged from the water. I recognized the whiskered snout, big eyes, and small-eared head of a sea lion. Although enormous, the animal moved smoothly and gracefully, but with great power. It resembled a California sea lion — the kind in aquarium shows — but it was lighter in color and much

bigger than I thought sea lions grew. It looked about as shy and good-natured as the average grizzly bear.

Then the animal roared. I remember that quite distinctly — it didn't bark, it *roared*. Its head was pulled back on its neck, and its mouth was open wide. I saw its yellow-brown teeth and was almost close enough to feel its hot, fishy breath.

How fragile our little boat seemed, when that was all that was separating us from the giant creature. Ken and I didn't stop to talk but paddled off without delay, as if our kayak had grown wings.

Today, however, I would be even closer to sea lions than that. And the only thing between us would be the water we shared. I earned my living now at Marine World (soon to become Marine World Africa USA), an oceanarium-zoo in Redwood City, California. This fifty-five-acre park was a very special place where visitors could see and learn to appreciate an astounding variety of animal life. In later years, exotic land animals such as chimpanzees, lions, elephants, and tigers would roam naturalistic jungle exhibits. But at this time, the park concentrated on ocean animals — fish and marine mammals that dived and swam in dozens of aquarium tanks. In Oceana Theatre, where I was now, there was a series of pens and pools housing killer whales and sea lions, plus a huge 650,000-gallon central pool where these creatures put on shows for park visitors.

I had taken a job at Marine World as a professional scuba diver. Wearing a rubber wetsuit, swimfins, and a face mask, I worked underwater every day. It was my job to clean the saltwater tanks where the dolphins, killer whales, and other creatures lived. Here algae, a primitive single-celled plant, could grow incredibly quickly. In a short time, the clinging slime could thicken on the tank floors and walls until it looked like a brown wool blanket. Then it would break off in chunks, dirtying the animals' water and blocking the visitors' views. So we divers scrubbed the stuff off with brushes, while enormous filtration machines sucked the loosened algae away.

The sea lions' tanks didn't need cleaning as often as those of the other animals. Because the pens had partial roofs over them, not much sunlight got through, and the shade slowed the growth of the algae. But on this particular day, the time had come to do the job. I had never gone in with the sea lions before, and I was a little nervous. Sea lions were so quick and maneuverable in the water, and I didn't think I'd be able to keep my eyes on them very well. Also, I couldn't help noticing their teeth, which were brown and ugly and sharp.

Still, cleaning the tanks was my job, I reminded myself. I had become a diver because I wanted to be near the creatures of the sea. Besides, one of the animal trainers had told me that even Nero, the biggest sea lion bull, was in a good mood that day.

To my left was an opening to the offstage sea lion pens. In front of me was Oceana Theatre, the gigantic pool where the killer whale and sea lion shows took place. A wave sloshed over my feet, and I turned to see the black and white bulk of a killer whale cruise by.

"Good morning, Yaka," I called. But the killer whale only glided on, silent in the morning light.

One step up to my right, behind a fenced walkway, I found a compressed-air outlet, one of many throughout the park. I plugged the brass fitting on the end of my airhose into the outlet. (The other end connected to my own scuba mouthpiece.) With a click and a *hissss,* compressed air rushed into the 100-foot coil of hose I had laid on the deck behind me. The yellow coils lifted and twisted, as if they were alive.

I gathered my courage and walked through the opening to the backstage sea lion pens. Here was a row of smaller pools fenced with forest-green mesh. Every pen had a half-roof to give its occupant the choice of sun or shade, a saltwater pool that extended beneath a redwood deck, and one or more sea lions.

After fastening my backpack straps, I swung the regulator hose over my shoulder. I tapped the metal mouthpiece on its end, sniffing briefly at the roar of released air. Any hint of an oily smell and I would have gone and changed the compressor filter; oil in the lungs can put you away. But all I could smell now was clean salt water, the faint bitter tang of the rubber tooth grip on the mouthpiece — and the animals themselves. Although the sea lions looked immaculately clean, their odor was powerful, like the smell of large dogs that have not been bathed in recent memory. And what a racket they made!

"Yarkyarkyarkyarkyarkyarkyark!"

The last pen held two small yearlings named Stan and Ollie. I figured I would start with them and work my way up through the larger ones to the pen of the biggest bull, Nero.

The yearlings posed no threat, of course. They weighed only about forty pounds each and were twelve to fourteen months old. This is the age when a show sea lion's training begins. In the wild, their mother would have been pushing them away about then, weaning them from her milk to fish that they caught themselves. They actually looked cute — big-eyed and a little shy. And, sure enough, when I slid up the gate latch to their pen, they leaped frantically from the deck into the water, their place of safety.

I closed the gate behind me and sat down on the edge of the deck with my legs dangling in the water. I adjusted my face mask — and slid into the water.

As always, there was the shock of sudden coolness as I slipped into an underwater world of palest blue. It was as though I swam in the sky. I loved the feeling of leaving land and gravity, of giving up the heavy thud, thud, thud of walking. Moving through the water was like flying — I could reach and glide and soar. And the water was so beautiful. That day, this section of the water was crystal clear. I watched the sunbeams touch the floor and dance in the water, the light patterns rippling, changing, inter-weaving.

The sea lion pools were next to those of the killer whales, the two areas separated by concrete walls to prevent the sea lions from becoming dinner. I rose to the surface for a moment and heard *PTOOOO-HUHHHP!* — the heavy, steamy sound that killer whales make when they breathe. Back underwater, I could feel the killer whales' unseen pres-ence. There were small square holes low in the walls between the pens, and water moved back and forth between them. When the killer whales in the nearby pens got excited and swam fast, the ripples from their movement surged into this pen.

Swoosh! The yearling sea lions were so quick that they were hard to see. Combining speed with total maneuverability, they cornered as if they had no bones. They could zip clean out of the water with one yank of their front flippers. Like all sea lions, they propelled themselves by tugging their flippers every so often in quick half breast-strokes, which sent them hurtling through the water.

I settled down to work. I was weighted for it, carrying about 45 pounds of lead on the canvas belt around my waist. We work divers had to be heavy so that we could scrub hard and not just push away from the floor.

The brush bit cleanly into the brown algae slime. I liked this kind of work. It was simple but vigorous, and it left the mind free to wander while the muscles exercised. Almost before I realized it, I was bumping against the far wall, and the pen was clean.

After I finished Stan and Ollie's pool, I did Gunther's. Next came the pen of Artemus, the smiling sea lion. The smile was something he had once done on his own, without being asked. His trainers had loved it and began to give him fish every time he did it. Now, of course, he smiled very often.

Time in these pools slipped by swiftly, almost without incident. Every once in a while I caught a glimpse of the sea lion who lived there, wheeling like a swift, dark gull above me. But mostly it was like being alone.

I told myself I had been worried for nothing.

At last I came to Nero's pen. Weighing in at about 400 pounds, Nero was the biggest sea lion in Oceana Theatre — *and* the most aggressive. When his pool needed cleaning, the trainers usually moved him temporarily to an empty pen. But that day, every pen was occupied by at least one sea lion.

I stood outside Nero's gate for a moment. Maybe I wanted to think about this. Also, something was in the way — the big bull sea lion leaned heavily against the gate, chest first. Some of his wet hair pushed through the mesh, and the gate sagged outward. The animal's mahogany-brown head bulged at the crest like a Mohawk haircut. His large brown eyes, rimmed in pure red, stared into my own. His whiskers were stiff, like yellow broom straws. As I watched, his cheek muscles flexed, and the whiskers moved forward. One of the animal trainers had told me this meant "Careful — don't mess with me!"

I had an uneasy feeling in my stomach. But the job still had to be done.

"Okay, Nero, I've got to clean your pen!" I said, talking loudly and pretend-cheerfully, more for myself than for Nero. I lifted up the sliding gate fastener, unlocking the mesh gate. I couldn't pull the gate backward toward me, because he might get out. So I pushed, expecting Nero to react with fright and hurry toward the water, as the others had done. Instead, he stayed where he was, pushing back as hard as I pushed in. He wouldn't budge.

"Uh — 'scuse me?" I said, pushing a little bit harder. "Would you mind moving back so I can . . ."

Nero ducked his head and looked around me. A trainer was passing by. The trainers controlled Nero's food and, as a result, controlled Nero. With a snort of apparent disgust at the coming of reinforcements, the dark brown creature abruptly turned away. He crossed the deck in one easy gallop and slipped into the water.

"Well, why didn't you do that in the first place?" I said. I stepped into the pen, not forgetting to close the gate behind me.

But Nero had not gone away. The deck had an air space underneath it, and I expected him to do as the other sea lions had done — duck back under the deck, out of my way. Then I could do my work quickly and leave. But this sea lion stayed next to the deck, right where I had to go in. I had to put my wetsuited legs and swimfinned bare ankles into the water right beside him.

I thought about how even show sea lions are basically wild animals. They're a little like hunting hawks, who will trade what they do for food or affection, but who never give up their wildness. Nero sniffed at my wetsuited knees. He didn't seem overly impressed with me. It crossed my mind that sea lions are distantly related to bears.

I actually had to shove him back with my swimfins just to get into the pool. Finally I slipped underwater.

Immediately there seemed to be half a dozen Neros in the pool. He buzzed me from every direction. How could anything move so fast, I thought. And every change of movement made a wall of water, a whirlwind I felt but could not see.

Wasting no time, I got down in my floor-scrubbing, push-up position and began to work. The water was a comfortably cool, soothing temperature, and my shoulders moved freely. The wetsuit I was wearing was called a "Farmer John." It was a sort of overall with pants that came up to the chest and over the shoulders, leaving the arms free to work. I was glad I didn't have my wetsuit jacket on.

That is, until Nero put his mouth on my bare forearm.

Up close, his eyes were brown except for that thin ring of crimson, which looked like the color of rage. His nostrils flared, snorting out bubbles, and their force against my skin felt as rough as windblown sand.

Then Nero wasn't there anymore. He had just vanished, as if he had never been there at all.

Suddenly, I wanted very badly to be finished. I scrubbed a little faster — well, maybe a whole lot faster!

Then Nero bit down on the seat of my pants. I felt sudden enormous pressure as the sea lion's jaws clamped down. He lifted me and shook me, violently, the way a dog breaks the neck of a rat. I tried to poke him with the scrub brush but missed. I heard a ripping sound as the cloth and rubber of my wetsuit tore, and for a second I thought that what was ripping was me. Cold water rushed into a place that had been warm and private before.

Then Nero pitched me aside, *thump!*, against the wall.

The animal was looking at me with those big, red-rimmed eyes. I could see the small, curled rolls of his ears, laid back. One side of his whiskers twitched, and his lip lifted.

I felt the skin on my face tighten. My cheeks turned hot. Embarrassment and anger filled me. I got my legs and feet underneath me — and leaped after him just as hard as I could.

I thumped him one good punch on the chest with the end of my scrub brush, and then Nero was in motion. Startled by my sudden loss of sanity, he allowed me to chase him for a while. But he was impossible to touch — I could only see blurs here and there as he sped by.

Then fatigue took the edge off my excitement. As my anger cooled and good sense returned, I realized I might not actually want to catch up with a 400-pound bull sea lion. I finally settled back on the floor and resumed scrubbing. I will not say I did a wonderful job, but I finished.

I clambered out of the pen — backward. When I was safely on the other side of the fencing, with the gate closed firmly between us, I told Nero in no uncertain terms exactly what I thought about him and all his relations.

Though my skin was not torn, and I was not hurt, my pants were spectacularly ripped. As I gathered my gear and walked away, I felt a distinct breeze — air conditioning where there was not supposed to be any. It was a long walk to the privacy of the dive shack, where I would find a spool of heavy-duty thread to sew the wetsuit closed.

I considered how many hundreds of people I would meet along the way, many of whom were likely to stare at someone who was dressed as strangely as I was. I paused to roll the top half of my wetsuit down, to cover the place that the lower half didn't.

As I walked on up toward the announcer's shack and the ring of trees that encircled Oceana, Nero's "Yarkyarkyark-yark!" followed me. I'm sure that he was only barking, telling the world that this was his territory. But to me that raucous voice held a ring of sarcastic laughter.

And this was before I had even heard of a giant sea lion named George.

2

Born in the Wild

It must have been about the time when Nero remodeled my wetsuit that George the Steller sea lion came into the world. His birthplace was a remote island in the icy waters of the Bering Sea. You can find it easily enough on a map. Just put your finger on Alaska's jutting tusk of land, and move it west until you come to a blue gap where the sea breaks through at Unimak Pass. Move north a couple of inches on the map (500 miles if you were in the water) and you will come to a group of tiny islands — actually extinct volcanoes — called the Pribilofs. One of these is the island of Saint George.

At the windward edge of this three-by-nine-mile island waves crash onto a gray rock beach. Below stark cliffs the rock, dotted here and there with shallow tide pools, slopes unevenly to the sea.

To this wild and windswept island come the largest sea lions in the world — Steller sea lions. They are named for a shipwrecked scientist, Georg Wilhem Steller, who first described them in 1742. These creatures come to Saint George every year, as they have for centuries. They swim for many miles along the Pacific shores on their journey from the south, where they spend the winter. In the spring, they arrive on the island to establish their rookery, or breeding colony. Here they will fight and mate and bear their young.

You can hear them from a mile away; their roaring is louder than the boom of the surf. And when you see them, it is almost as if the long-dead volcano has erupted and overflowed once more. Everywhere you look there is the movement of golden brown bodies over the rocks.

In appearance, Steller sea lions resemble their close cousins, the California sea lions (the ones at Marine World). Both are members of the same group of marine mammals — the pinnipeds — which includes sea lions, seals, and walruses. But the two belong to different species: the Steller sea lion has the scientific name *Eumetopias jubata;* the California sea lion is *Zalophus californianus.* Stellers' coloration is lighter and more varied than that of the California sea lions; it can be red-gold, cinnamon, copper, or blond. But it is their size more than anything that sets Stellers apart from their cousins. Stellers are huge. Nero, Marine World's biggest trained California sea lion, weighed 400 pounds. A full-grown Steller bull can easily weigh more than five times that much — up to 2,200 pounds! The females, or cows, are much smaller, but even they can tip the scales at 600 to 800 pounds. The enormous creature that appeared at the side of our kayak on that day in Half Moon Bay was almost certainly a Steller.

The first Stellers to arrive on the island each year are the bulls. They come three weeks before the cows do, which is a good thing, since the bulls arrive ready to fight among themselves. Their dangerous battles must be pretty much over before the cows arrive and the vulnerable babies are born.

The bulls are tremendous fighters. Soon after birth they start to "train" for the mighty battles they will fight to win a piece of land — a territory that they hope will attract females. The reason for this rivalry is mating. The females will mate once, and only once, each season. When that moment for mating finally arrives — well, the bulls want to be where the cows are! Since the females wander wherever they choose, the bulls try to claim the territory the cows are most likely to want. It may be a stretch of rock close enough to the water for easy exit. Or perhaps it is one with a nice ridge of rock to give a new baby shelter from the sun. Certain territories on the island are especially desirable. These are picked first, with the most powerful bulls claiming the same places year after year. And so the bulls fight. Only the strongest earn the right to reproduce, therefore keeping the species strong.

We cannot know exactly how George was born and lived during his earliest days, for no human eye was there to see. But from accounts of other Alaskan Stellers that have been observed, we can get a good idea of how it might have happened.

In late spring 1972, a certain pregnant female Steller came

ashore on the island of Saint George. Her pregnant condition was given away only by a slight thickening in the lower portion of her muscular body, and perhaps by the faintest slowing of her motion. She was the picture of health, with a hint of new-penny copper in her cinnamon-colored fur. The 750-pound mother-to-be growled and nipped at a couple of females to make them move aside. Then she settled down to wait.

One morning when the mist was lifting from the sea, she suddenly seemed to go berserk.

"HHHAAAHHHHHH!" she hissed, spinning, then arching her neck back. She bared her teeth and, trembling with energy, yanked herself into the forward threat position. Her head went down on her chest; her neck reared back, ready to strike.

The other females immediately understood and gave way, clearing a space five or six feet wide in all directions. They knew she was about to give birth to her pup. And that it could mean a fierce fight if they got in her way. In the center of the circle, the almost-mother labored hard. Often, during brief periods of rest, she looked back toward her tail area. She made a soft, almost questioning sound, "AHRR-rrrr?" as the pup slowly began to emerge. It was her pup-attraction cry — a special call she would give to him, and no other, during his babyhood.

Then, with a final surge of effort by the mother, the sea lion that would one day be known as George was born. His mother nuzzled him, sniffed him, and tickled him with her broom-straw whiskers. George lifted his little head and opened his pink-lined mouth.

But no sound came out. His lungs were still full of fluid.

The umbilical cord had broken when he came out, and that meant he was getting no oxygen. He was alive but not breathing.

The mother reached down and picked him up by the loose skin across his shoulders. She lifted him several feet off the ground — and dropped him.

George choked and spluttered. He cried, "Maa-aa-aa!" His mother was satisfied; her baby was breathing. If he had not done so, she would have picked him up and dropped him again and again, forty or fifty times if need be, until he cleared his lungs. For exactly the same reason, human doctors used to give a newborn baby a smack on the seat or the soles of the feet, to make him or her yell, and breathe, and live.

By human standards, George was hardly a little baby. At birth he already weighed nearly fifty pounds and was three-and-a-half feet long. His baby coat of fur was dark brown, glinting with silver. As he grew and matured, his coloration would change to brown, then cinnamon, and finally to a splendid buff, or whitish gold.

Steam rose from the newborn's wet fur. George felt the forty-degree weather keenly, but surprisingly he did not shiver. Underneath his dark fur and hide, George had a special kind of "baby fat," different from the layers of blubber that kept the adults warm in the near-freezing sea. George had been warm enough inside his mother's body. Now that the air was chill around him, the special baby fat would keep George from getting *too* cold — but only for a while. He needed to build some thick blubber quickly, and this physical need made him hungry! He waggled his head back and forth clumsily, crying out his baby cry.

George's mother knew he wanted to be fed, but there was something else to be done first. Once more she opened her mouth, leaned very close, and made her special sound, "AHRR-rrrr!" It was the same sound she had made before, but louder — so loud that, for George, it drowned out all other noises of the rookery. The gulls' screams, the roars of the bulls, the bleating wails of other pups, the crash of the surf — all these were drowned out from George's hearing so that he could concentrate on that one special sound.

It was vital that George know his mother's call. In a week or two, when she went to sea to hunt for food, she would have no choice but to leave George. There was no way he could keep up with the fast-and-fancy swimming she would have to do to run down fish to eat. When she returned, she would call George to her. If he approached the wrong mother, this mother might defend her own baby's food supply by biting or throwing George violently. So he had to recognize his own mother's call.

For fifteen minutes this important "conversation" continued. "AHRR-rrrr!" "Maa-aaa!" "AHRR-rrrr!" "Maa-aaa!"

Then at last George's mother picked him up once more, by the skin across his shoulders. But this time she didn't drop him. Instead she leaned back, placed the pup on her belly, and nudged him with her flipper.

Nobody had to tell George what to do next. He was born knowing certain things, and nuzzling in the warm fur of his mother's chest was part of this instinctive knowledge. He was hunting for something. His mother's flipper guided him, and presently the search was rewarded as a small black nipple, one of six, rose up.

George greedily sucked in the warm milk. White and thick, it was heavy with fat and protein the pup needed to build muscle and blubber. He drank, lost his grip, and found it again. His mother nudged him whenever he stopped slurping the thick, rich stuff.

For forty-five minutes the feeding continued, until George had so much in his stomach that he couldn't swallow it right away. He kept the milk in his bulging cheeks awhile before forcing it down his throat. He wanted to keep eating but had no place to put it!

His mother kept forcing him, and George's belly swelled rounder and rounder. Finally he hiccuped, belched, and threw up. This seemed to satisfy his mother; an overflowing pup was really full. George's little head slumped down, and this time his mother let him sleep.

Two hours later, George twitched, stirred, and started to lift his head. The instant that he woke, his mother's eyes flicked down to him. She watched him for a moment to see what he would do.

George's head lost coordination and flopped down abruptly, like a puppet whose strings were cut. But then George raised his head again and turned over, still on his mother's stomach.

A newborn human would not have been strong enough for even such a gentle adventure as turning over for several months. But George was born ready to go — and it was a good thing, too, for his was no gentle world. From the instant of birth he was threatened with danger from land, sea, and sky. Danger came from seagulls that might attack him with their sharp beaks; from other, larger animals such as killer whales; and from storms at sea. Luckily, nature had given him built-in tools to swim and fight with. Now, if he could just figure out how to use what he had. . . .

George sniffed at one black, rubbery front flipper. He waved it uncertainly. He noticed he had another one just like it. He wobbled his left flipper and then his right. George didn't know it yet, but these short, strong flippers were to him what wings are to a bird. He was built to become one of the greatest "fliers" of the underwater world. Experimentally, George touched the backs of his two front flippers together, then separated them, instinctively breaststroking in the air. It was a special moment, like a human baby's first step. He was imitating the swim stroke that would one day send him hurtling through the water.

Then George felt hungry again and nudged his mother's broad, brown chest. She stroked him with her own great flipper, nuzzled him softly — and dumped him on the rocks. George cried out and tried to climb back onto the warm and comfortable softness. But his mother backed away from him. All George could do was follow, crying as he shuffled awkwardly along.

His mother called out the pup-attraction sound and moved backward again, away from her newborn. George followed until he came to a ridge in the rock. Then he stopped. The six-inch rise was a lot of hill for little George to climb. His mother nudged him once toward the ridge, to be sure he understood. She barked, using a different tone than George had heard before — it was a command. When George still didn't move, his mother nipped him sharply on the back end. That made him climb the ridge in a hurry!

Moving away and calling her pup, George's mother

backed up in a large circle, leading them back to where they had begun. Only then did George get fed.

Every couple of hours that first day, George's mother made him exercise, and each time she made it a little tougher. Avoiding crowds of other females, she snarled horribly at any who came near. She called George up a slope, which was, to him, much too steep. His small, new flippers were sore from crawling on the rough-surfaced rocks, but he did as he was told. Now he recognized his mother's bark — the sound that had "teeth" in it.

His mother wasn't being cruel. She knew what George could not know: about summer storms, and waves that swept up and dragged young pups away. If the sea should reach up and take hold of George now, she wanted him strong enough to clutch on to a rock and survive, or to run a few steps farther up on the beach to get out of reach of the waves.

For the first two weeks, she never left him, not even to fish for food. She lived on her reserves of fat, and George lived on her milk. She hardly took her eyes off her pup.

One of the greatest dangers newborn pups faced was from the bulls. When these moving mountains of muscle fought, any pup in the way could be crushed. It wasn't the bulls' fault; their hides were so thick they couldn't feel something as small and soft as a pup underneath them when they were in the heat of battle.

Although the territories were by now firmly established and there were far more threats than actual fighting, the possibility of violence would be there until the last bull left in late August. They were under continuous tension, these mountainous bulls. They rocked back and forth on their flippers, roaring their threats and making the motions of battle.

Sea lion property was marked out either by some natural boundary, such as a ridge of rock, or by an invisible but clearly understood line. If any bull took one shuffling step onto another's territory, the invaded bull's whiskers would rise and flex forward. That was a warning. If the trespasser advanced another inch, the defending bull would hurl himself flat on the ground, flippers behind him, neck outstretched. This was warning number two. Then the defender would rear back up, ready to strike for real. If the other bull backed away, all would be well. If not, there would be war.

During the six to eight weeks the bulls were ashore, they slept very little and didn't eat at all. They might lose 600 pounds on this starvation diet. If one left his "property" to go for a swim, another bull might take his spot, and the fighting would have to be done all over again.

George was growing and learning rapidly. At first he pulled himself along with his front flippers, dragging his hindquarters. But as he grew, his motion changed, so that he used all four flippers. Now he carried his chest and shoulders high, rocking from side to side, as if to say, "Get out of my way!"

Sea lion pups are wonderfully curious and active, and George was no exception. He picked up pebbles in his mouth, tossed them, and then hurried to pick them up again. He also began to discover the other male and female pups who were part of his pup pod, or group. The pups played together in a safe area where the bulls did not often go. (It was in the middle of a territory, and the bulls' fights were mainly at the territorial borders.)

With each passing day, George became more and more confident of his own abilities and was sometimes less than eager to come running when his mother called. Then one day something happened that showed him why he needed to listen to her commands and steer clear of the bulls.

The incident began with a small moving dot, visible far out at sea. It came steadily closer and closer, until it became recognizable as a late-arriving, full-grown Steller bull. He was dark brown, the color of strong coffee, and huge — with more than a ton of muscle. Heavy scars across his head, neck, and chest showed that he had fought before, many times, and had not run away.

The year before, the place where George now played had been part of the coffee-colored bull's territory, and he had fully intended to take it again. But he had been delayed. Now he was back in his home waters, already in a foul mood because he should have been mating by this time. Then he saw it — *someone was in his territory!*

Usually, late-arriving bulls wait in the shallows and roar for a while, threatening, working up their courage for a mad dash up the beach. But the dark bull had no time for such delay.

He charged in from the surf, roaring. He came galloping through the other bulls' territories so swiftly that the bulls could not react quickly enough to stop him.

The tawny gold bull who had taken over the coffee-colored bull's territory saw the dark bull coming. He was not slow to answer. He was fully as huge as the coffee bull, and just as ready to fight. But he was young and inexperienced, and he committed a tactical error. He should have stayed where he was, holding the higher ground and making the older bull fight up the hill against gravity. But he was too excited and came down the slope, bellowing in his eagerness to get at his rival. Both bulls were now so worked up they could see nothing but each other.

And in between the charging bulls was puppy George.

His mother spotted the danger at once and barked furiously at him. But George was involved with an interesting bit of driftwood just then and was too busy to respond. He heard the noise, but the bulls were always loud anyway. So he paid no attention to the onrushing giants. He picked up the wood in his mouth.

Too late he sensed that something unusual was happening. He looked to his left to see the great golden mass bearing down on top of him. If he stayed where he was, he'd be crushed, and there was no time to run.

But a slender neck reached out, and George's mother snatched him. In one motion she picked him up and threw him, flinging him out of death's way just as the two bulls crashed together.

In violent combat they fought, heads striking and dodging so swiftly the eye could not follow. Sometimes one grasped the other and bit and shook, roaring horribly over the mouthful of muscle and hide. Shoving, biting, and roaring, trying for each other's faces and flippers, they fought. The huge bulls heaved their chests against each other, trying to wrestle the other one back. The dark bull faked a jab at the golden bull's face, then dived for his flipper — but that, too, was only a feint. When the younger bull snatched away his flipper and lunged back with open mouth to make his own attack, the dark bull took his real target. He seized the golden bull by the neck, just below the jaw, and lifted with a surge of incredible strength. He heaved the entire mass of the younger bull's body over his shoulder, flinging him down.

The golden bull tried to get up and fight, but the coffee bull bit him half a dozen times in quick succession — snap!snap!snap!snap! The young bull was so confused he could not even make the surrender signals (several rapid lunges of the head toward the victor's lower jaw). He could only roll and try to get away. He scrambled and fled, and the older bull let him go, stopping his attack at the edge of his land. Then the dark bull turned and roared "ORRRRR!" at everyone else, just to let them know he was back and in command.

As the golden bull fought his way down to the beach, he had a hard time of it. The other bulls had their own territories all worked out and did not want the young bull taking over. So now they bit and roared and chased him until he slumped, bloody and exhausted, into the cooling surf. He would be all right. His body was built to handle such roughness; his hide and blubber were thick and sturdy, and his wounds would heal. Like all defeated bulls, he would just live for a while on the "bachelor beach," a stretch of shore for bulls too old or too young to hold a piece of land. Next year, he would try again to win and hold his own territory.

As for George, after that he stayed clear of the bulls and came more swiftly when his mother called. But at the same time, his playing, and that of the other male pups, began to include imitations of the bulls' behavior.

One day a tough little pup came up to George and pushed against him. George shoved back and growled, and the two muscled each other back and forth for a minute. Then both ran off together. After this, each time George woke up from a nap he went immediately to the pup pod — after he was finished getting fed, of course!

And then one afternoon, George discovered something on which his whole life would be centered. The other pups were stepping into a large pool in the rocks. George was curious and approached the deep splash pool. His mother followed as George bent down and touched his muzzle to the water. His tongue went out and he tasted the bitter tang of salt water. This was not milk!

Then George's mother shouldered past him into the pool and barked at him. George hesitated. But he recognized the command, and besides, he was a little hungry. (George was always at least a little hungry.) He leaned forward again and carefully put his nose to the rippling surface. The water moved and was cold. He flexed his nostrils open (unlike human noses, sea lions' noses are closed tight when relaxed and have to be opened on purpose). George sniffed in some water. It went up his nose and he choked.

His mother called to him again. George took a couple of hesitant steps — and then turned and ran. With a loud bark, his mother charged up the slope and picked George up by the back. She returned to the water and moved out till she was chest deep and George was floundering and splashing just above the water. Then she let go.

George was born knowing how to swim. But he didn't *know* that he knew how to swim. The salt water broke beneath his falling weight and closed over him. George tried to breathe and could not. He pumped his front flippers frantically and wiggled his bottom half uselessly. He didn't know that the rear flippers were for steering, the front ones for power. He flopped and splashed and held his head and long neck as high out of the water as he could, which of course made him work twice as hard.

Still, he made it to shore. He was safe! Until his mother came and grabbed him and threw him in again. But she also nuzzled him underwater. (Between a sea lion mother and pup, nose-to-nose contact means comfort and reassurance.) She half-supported George with her flippers, but the instant he stopped crying out, she let him sink again.

At last they compromised. George wanted to be fed, and his mother wanted him beside her in the water, where he had to learn to be comfortable. So when he had struggled to shore for about the twelfth time, she followed him almost in. She rolled on her side and waited in the shallows. If he wanted some food, he had to come and get it. At last, the attraction of stuffing his stomach won out. George waded out and clambered up onto his mother. After a few such feedings, he learned to be at home in the water, and the splash pools became enjoyable places for him.

One day George climbed up on a small rock in the middle of the splash pool, and another pup came up behind him and pushed George off. George tumbled into the water, rushed right back up, and shoved the first pup off. Then he turned to challenge everybody.

Once he had discovered this "game," George began to

swim more and more. Now he swam on his own much harder than he would have if his mother had forced him. He was soon one of the strongest young pups in the pod. When he climbed to the top of the rock in the pool and roared his miniature roar, the others would climb up the slope, and George would fling them down. He became almost impossible to dislodge. He'd crouch and make head motions like the big bulls did. Then he'd use his weight to lean on his opponents and tire them out. He could sometimes throw off ten or eleven challengers before he got too out of breath and collapsed backward into the cooling waters.

By this time, George was about a month old. He fairly dominated the pup pod — unless the yearlings came around. These year-old sea lions were natural bullies and often made life miserable for the month-old pups. But that was just the way of the sea lion community.

As the weeks passed, adventures happened, large and small. George watched from the shore when the killer whales came. He saw how a bull was surrounded and caught. The bull was hit by the killer whale's great flukes and tossed clear out of the water, falling back dazed. Just one solid hit was all it took, and when the bull fell he was crunched between the giant jaws and was gone. George also watched as a pup about his size was snatched off a rock by another killer whale. That whale threw its black and white body halfway up onto the land to grab the pup.

Once a summer storm arose, and the huge waves swept away many pups. But George's mother took him to high ground. She got into two fights along the way. One was with another female who was equally anxious to get her own pup to safety. Another was with a bull who got excited by the storm and wanted to mate. But she won out over both (the bull got his face bitten!), and George and his mother sat out the storm in safety.

So in his first month of life, George grew and prospered. He was beginning to learn how to take care of himself. And if he couldn't, well, there was always his ferocious mother, who would come running to straighten things out.

But all too soon, the most dangerous enemy would come — one against which even George's ferocious mother could offer no protection at all.

3
Caught!

*T*he first warning came from the gulls.

The Western grayback seagulls always gave a certain raucous cry when humans came near. To the gulls, the humans often meant food — scraps of fishing bait or pieces of the animals or fish they had killed.

When the sea lions heard the gulls begin to scream, they fled for the sea, for their lives. Bulls, cows, yearlings — in seconds the rocks were bare, leaving only the pups. From the center of the pup pod, George lifted his head and blinked. The adults were all galloping frantically for the water. George and the other pups cried out, their round eyes huge, their small mouths yawping. But their mothers could not help them. Even the most dedicated Steller mother would not be able to swim long while grasping a dog-sized pup in her mouth.

And then the humans came.

It might seem strange for these enormous animals to be afraid of three humans in a boat. In a fair fight, any half-grown bull there could have destroyed the strongest man. The bulls could have handled the invaders just by moving over them and crushing them.

Strangely, though, even in the early days of sea lion slaughter, the bulls had never killed people. A furious bull would chase an invader to the edge of his territory, but no farther. Even against each other, the Stellers never seemed to fight to the death. When one fighting bull decided to give up, he moved his head in the surrender signal, and the other bull let him leave.

The sea lions put limits on their violence, but for many years the humans did not.

For a hundred years or more, seals and sea lions had been killed without restraint. Humans had used pistols, rifles, shotguns, machine guns, and even small bombs and hand grenades, as well as clubs, swung like baseball bats, to crush an animal's skull.

The killers had their reasons — all of them based on greed and/or misconceptions. Fishermen falsely believed that the Stellers were robbing them of their catch by eating too much fish. Bounty hunters killed the animals for their scalps or ears, which could be sold. The Stellers were also killed for sale to people who believed wrongly that drugs made from parts of the Stellers' bodies would keep them strong and virile. And, like the North American bison, the Steller was simply a challenge to hunters who enjoyed killing such huge creatures for sport.

At first, the giant sea lions had been easy to kill because they had not learned to fear people. Any scrawny hunter with a gun could just walk up and shoot a bull protecting his hard-won territory, or club a female's brains out if she stayed by her pup. The slaughter had been unbelievable — whole rookeries destroyed, down to the last animal. The Stellers learned that to stay and defend a pup or a territory was useless; to do so meant only that the whole sea lion community would be destroyed. To survive, the Stellers had learned to run from the humans and their guns. Now even the sharp crack of a falling rock would sometimes stampede them to the sea. So when three men in a boat arrived on Saint George Island, George's mother fled to the sea, along with the other females. Then, from the water she watched, straining to see what was happening. But her nearsighted vision showed only blurs as the men walked among the sea lion pups too young to get away.

She couldn't see what the men were doing when they leaned over and, with expert hands, lifted the pups one by one, setting them down into wire cages. She also didn't see when one of the men nodded at George and another bent down and took him.

Even as the boat pulled away, she rushed back up the gray rock beach, hurrying to the place where she usually met George. She charged up to any pup she found by itself, calling, "AHRR-rrrr? AHRR-rrrr?" And when she sniffed and knew it was not hers, she seized it and flung it aside.

For three weeks more she stayed close to their meeting

place, calling and calling, "AHRR-rrrr? AHRR-rrrr?" She investigated every pup that wandered near.

But she never saw George again.

Lifted by his tail flippers, George was put into a wire basket and taken to the boat. Ten pups were taken, and in ten wire cages they made the boat ride to the mainland. The cages, with their bawling occupants, were then transferred to a truck.

The truck was a big one, like the parcel-post trucks that mail carriers use, with a rolltop door at one end. One by one, the pups were lifted up in their cages and set onto the sand-covered truck bed. George was used to having rock underneath him, so the two inches of sand pushing up into the bottom of the cage felt soft and comfortable — it was the softest thing George had ever touched, except for his mother.

The door rolled shut, blocking out the sun. The truck motor growled to a start. Then the sounds of the sea went away.

The humans who had taken George were not out to hurt or kill sea lions. They were collectors, working with a permit to capture animals for zoos. A new Marine Mammal Protection Act was about to go into effect, and it would soon be extremely difficult to get a permit to catch sea lions for any reason, including public display. But at this time it could still be done legally.

The collectors did their best to handle and transport the Steller pups with care. For two days and nights they drove, stopping only to change drivers and get gas. They sprayed the pups down with a water hose when the gas stations had one, but aside from that, there wasn't much they could do to give the pups any comfort. They knew it was best just to get them where they were going as fast as they could.

Fortunately the collectors knew enough not to carry the pups in canvas sacks with only their heads sticking out. That had been done in the past, when Steller pups had been captured for experimentation. Stellers can't stand being tied up like that, and those little pups had fought the bags the whole way. Some struggled so long and hard that they died from overheating.

George was not fed on the trip, but that was no problem — at least not right away. At his age, he could go as long as a week without suffering ill effects from hunger. In the wild, he might have had to wait that long while his mother went out to sea to hunt for her own food. Mostly, he and the other pups just slept, except when the road was too rough. Then they got sick to their stomachs and bawled, and some threw up.

At long last, the door at the back of the truck opened. George blinked at the creaking noise and the sudden light. He didn't know it, but his future was about to be decided. The truck had come to a stop at Marine World. According to an earlier agreement, the collectors were giving two of the Steller pups to the park. A couple of people from the park were waiting to take the pups.

The truck bed swayed as the men climbed aboard. "I'll take that one, and that one," said one of them. And George and another pup — a female — were lifted in their wire cages and handed off the truck.

The caged pups were taken to a large enclosure called Seal Compound. It was surrounded by a high green chain-link fence. Inside, the floor was smooth concrete. A ramp led to an oversized bathtub filled with fresh water. The concrete floor would be comfortable for the pups, since they were used to rock. There was even a raised area on the floor where they could sun themselves.

The two pups hesitated a bit before leaving the wire cages — even the cages were more familiar than the unknown. But presently George stepped timidly out onto the concrete. There was a slanting runway up to the little tub, and he did not need to be told what to do. As if he had been doing it for years, he clambered up the runway. Then he stopped and sniffed at the surface of the strange-smelling water. It was chlorinated, and George had never smelled chlorine before. But as with all the other new things he was about to encounter, he soon got used to it. The female pup came out of her cage, too, and together the two began to investigate their new surroundings.

Later that day, a small group of Marine World technicians and helpers gathered at the pups' pen. Veterinarians Ron Swallow and Stan Searles, handlers Ed Comer and Dee "Rags" Cross, and animal caretaker John Benner watched the two pups with a mixture of delight and concern. They knew that the pups, who had by now been named George and Eleanor (after Senator McGovern and his wife), needed to be fed. Although they would have preferred not to, they also knew that they would have to use a stomach tube to do the job. Shoving a plastic tube down the pups' throats and into their stomachs would be uncomfortable for everybody — especially for George and Eleanor. But it was the only way to do it.

Other scientists had tried many other methods for feeding Steller pups in captivity. Almost all had been unsuccessful. In one long-ago experiment, eighty Steller pups had been rescued where they had washed up on the rocks after a storm. (They would have died without their mothers.) The rescuers had tried every way they could think of to get a special milk formula into the pups. They had tried bottles with many different kinds of nipples, and liquid food that they dribbled onto their fingers. They had even tried pouring the formula onto the pups' flipper joints, because it had been observed that Steller pups frequently suck on each other's flippers the way a human baby might suck on a thumb or pacifier. But that didn't work either. In that sad experiment, seventy-three of the eighty pups died because they wouldn't accept food by any of these methods. Eventually, people figured out that they should stick with tube feeding. Nobody liked it, but it got the food down.

Now the Marine World people approached the pen with the feeding equipment. Eleanor backed away, but George sniffed the air to both the right and left. He then began to shuffle slowly back and forth, swinging his shoulders and hips widely, so that everyone would know what an extremely ferocious animal he was.

"You're a bad dude, all right, George," said big, gentle John Benner (J.B.), with a smile. "We've got to get some food into you, okay? You're not gonna like it. But it's the only way."

Then the men entered the pen, and George backed up quickly beside Eleanor.

"We're not gonna hurt you, I promise," said J.B. softly.

"You want to hold him?" asked Ron Swallow. He began

to apply petroleum jelly to the first couple feet of the long coil of one-inch plastic hose. That way, it would slide more easily down George's throat.

"Yeah," said J.B. He laid down an old piece of beat-up wrestling mat, moving slowly so as not to frighten the pup. Then he reached slowly over to George and picked him up as if he were a human baby, under the armpits. George's head moved swiftly and J.B. let him go, bright spots of blood showing on his hand.

"That was not nice, you bad boy, George!" he said, shaking his unwounded hand at the infant sea lion.

Forewarned, J.B. next grasped George at the back of his muscled neck, lifting him unceremoniously onto the yellow wrestling mat.

J.B. left to clean up his wounds, and strong, wiry Ed Comer took his place, kneeling across the struggling pup's body. Working quickly but carefully, Ed took hold of the slack scruff of hair and hide on the underside of George's jaw. He did not have to open the jaws. George took care of that, trying so hard to bite that his eyes bulged and the white ring around his eyeballs showed in fear and frustrated rage. Dee Cross got another grip at the back of George's neck. Then, with Stan Searles assisting Ron Swallow, they slowly pushed the slippery end of the plastic hose between George's small, sharp teeth.

George tried to bite but couldn't. He tried to vomit up the hose, but he couldn't do that, either. Frightened and uncomfortable, he fought every inch of the way as the slippery thing was shoved down his throat, all the way into his stomach.

Then Ron poured some gray glop from a pitcher into a

funnel set in the end of the tube. The glop was a highly nutritious mixture of blenderized mackerel, whipping cream, soy powder, and vitamins. It was as much like a Steller mother's milk as possible. Presently George's belly swelled noticeably.

The vet removed the funnel from the high end of the tube. He put his mouth around the end of the hose and blew into it, pushing the last bit of liquid food into George.

"Okay, I'm through," he said.

Gently the workers extracted the tube. George hiccuped softly, and everybody grinned. Then George vomited spectacularly, spraying gray glop on everything and everybody within range.

"Can't we just give him a bottle?" somebody asked plaintively, when the laughter and good-natured cursing had died down.

"I have good news and bad news," said Ron Swallow. "The bad news is we have to start all over."

"And what's the good news?"

"The good news is we only have to do this four times a day."

"For how long?"

"Until they eat solid food on their own — six months, maybe a year — who knows?"

4

George Makes Himself at Home

One morning a few months later, as the early light chased shadows from the pups' pen, Eleanor lifted her head. She looked at George, still snuggled up asleep beside her. Experimentally she nipped at his flipper. George opened his mouth, but his eyes remained determinedly shut.

Next, Ellie rolled over and back again, and slapped her flipper against George's back. He made a noise. His muscles started to tense up. He snorted a small hissing sigh, and then let his body relax back into sleep.

Even now, at six months of age, the pups had personalities that were already revealing themselves. George much preferred to let the morning sunshine enter the pen unnoticed, so that the gentle beams warmed him and woke him gradually. Ellie, on the other hand, was full of mischief and always ready to play the minute the stars had faded.

George was almost never the one to start the day's excitement. He had tremendous energy once he got going, and at 100 pounds, he was already a bit larger and stronger than Ellie. But it took him a while to become playful. So when Ellie nudged him, he showed his teeth again, threatening.

Ellie waited another thirty seconds. Then she stealthily gathered her flippers underneath her, getting ready to move fast. She positioned her teeth around, but not touching, George's limp flipper, as its owner slept on. Then, all in one motion, she bit, lifted, and dragged, hauling George's whole body six inches over the concrete.

George woke with a roar. Maybe it still came out more like an "Urrrr!" than the "AOUWRRRR" of the great bulls, but his intent was clear. Up on all fours he sprang, head back and eyes glaring, so that the white rings around his eyeballs showed. Neck back, muscles flexed, all teeth bared, his whole posture threatened nothing less than murder!

Ellie rushed up the ladder to the tub. George chased her all the way up the slide and into the chilly water. Then the fun really began, as the two pups rolled and plunged and tumbled in their self-made waves. In and out of the water they raced. George always chased Ellie. Sometimes she turned and hissed at him, lashing her open mouth back and forth. George appeared to regard this as an invitation, and he moved in to shove his chest against hers. He drove her back and down the ladder, leaning with his greater strength before she at last nipped his shoulder sharply, calling a halt when he was just getting warmed up. Then George

lumbered back down to the concrete and, crouching, began to practice his fighting skills.

Practice-fighting was something all young male Stellers did in the wild. Pups, yearlings, and subadults alike went through thousands of fake fights, readying themselves for the great duels they would fight as adult bulls. There were certain moves George practiced every day. Some he knew by instinct — they were part of his inborn "knowledge." Others he worked out for himself, or perhaps remembered from watching bulls in the wild. He always began his fighting drills on all fours, in the balanced "push-up" position sea lions use when ready to attack. His belly was off the ground, his neck pulled back like a cobra ready to strike.

Then he would lunge forward, slamming his chest and belly — *thump!* — against the ground. It looked as if it should hurt, he hit the ground so hard. But his thick fur and hide were tough — a natural shield. In time he would also have a mane of thick hair around his neck and chest, which, like that of the African lion, would help to absorb blows and bites.

The lunges George practiced were essential for fighting. In a real fight, when George would dive for an opponent's flipper to try to bite and cripple him, he would begin by hurling himself flat. He had to be comfortable in that position. He also needed to have the strength to get up instantly if he should miss his grab. This was important because when flat on the ground, he left his whole neck and back exposed to the teeth of his rival. The lunge was also important for developing power for the chest-to-chest shoving matches which sometimes settled fights before they really began.

After thirty or forty lunges and falls, George practiced his biting moves. The head and neck of a fighting sea lion must act and react as swiftly as a boxer's fist, with lightning moves, countermoves, and combinations. Biting itself is not difficult, but enemies seldom hold still and let themselves be bitten. Where and how the bite is applied is tremendously important. George's favorite combination was three false "jabs" to the side of the opponent's neck, followed by a sudden and serious lunge to the opponent's flipper.

Ellie was not much interested in these practice drills. Females could fight if necessary to establish an area for giving birth or to protect a pup. But in the wild, the tremendous battles of the bulls played no part in their lives. They were something to keep pups safe from, and to avoid.

While George practiced his moves, Ellie made up little games involving objects in the pen. That day, she hustled up a small round pebble and flipped it back and forth on the ground before her, like a miniature hockey puck. Another time, she and George had found a dead snake and played with it delightedly for hours — until the "toy" fell apart. (Whether the snake was found dead or was killed by the pups was never entirely clear.)

A seagull flapped onto the green fencing, looking for some leftover fish. Spying some in the corner, the gray-and-white scavenger settled to the floor and began to peck. George immediately did his territorial defense duty by roaring. Chest out, he stalked back and forth and showed all his terrible baby teeth. But the gull knew a pup when it saw one and paid him no mind.

Clump, clump, clump. The seagull fluttered quickly to the fence at the sound of an approaching human.

George and Ellie instantly became excited, leaving the pebble and the practice-fighting. Not long before, they had discovered two small square pieces of white plastic set nose-high in the fence. When the two pups had investigated these objects, a whistle had sounded, and food, in the form of whole fish, had been tossed over the fence to them.

The pups no longer needed to be tube-fed, having learned to take their fish straight. Over the past months the handlers had gradually increased the amount of fish in the pups' formula. Then they had progressed to pushing one whole fish, then two, down George and Ellie's throats. Finally, trainers tossed whole fish to the pups. At first, George and Ellie were not quite sure what to do with these shining creatures that didn't move or swim. But one day, Ellie tossed up a silver herring and caught it in her mouth. She bit once and swallowed, as though she had been doing it for years. George watched for a moment — and then followed her example. After that, the stomach tube was laid aside for good, and the pups could fully enjoy their meals.

They quickly learned that pressing their noses to the white plastic squares on the fence would always bring the small, sweet cry of the whistle, and then food. Although they had no way of knowing it, this was the beginning of their training.

For Marine World was not only an oceanarium where wild animals could be seen, it was also a stage where they performed. At Marine World we wanted visitors to see our animals at their athletic best — to watch them show off the skills they used in the wild. This was difficult. We couldn't show a sea lion hurtling through the sea after a school of live fish, or a killer whale battling a storm. Instead, we trained the animals to do special moves, such as flips and leaps, that would both entertain people and give them an idea of the animals' natural agility and strength.

We wanted our guests to go away loving and respecting the creatures of the sea as much as we did. No matter what silly hats and costumes our trainers and announcers might wear, everything the *animals* did in our shows was taken from their natural behavior. There were no "tricks." (Trainers hate the word *trick,* which implies deception; they use the word *behavior* instead.) The behaviors had to be comfortable for the animals or, after a while, they would simply refuse to perform.

Training any animal was not easy; with show animals the job was doubly difficult. It required long hours of practice, with trainer and animal working closely together. California sea lions had long been favorites for this because they were active, curious, and cooperative — as long as the fish kept coming. But to train an aggressive Steller sea lion bull, which might grow to more than ten times the weight of the trainer — *that* was a somewhat larger challenge.

Since I was a diver and not an animal trainer, I knew that I, personally, wouldn't be the one to try the experiment. But I was fascinated by the Stellers and by the training process in general, so I followed George's progress with interest. I learned everything I could about Stellers and their training. Like everyone at Marine World, I was curious to see what would happen.

Around the world, a handful of people had tried to train Stellers, but the results were not encouraging. Since people naturally like to talk more about their successes than their failures, not much was said about Stellers. "Too big, too aggressive," the trainers would say if you spoke to them privately. One park had had Stellers but had gotten rid of them for these very reasons.

Stellers were most certainly not pets. There were plenty of stories to confirm that. One boat captain in Alaska had apparently thought to make a "pal" out of a Steller bull that had appeared beside his boat. The captain threw fish and the animal liked it, and everything was fine until the man ran out of fish. Then the Steller got angry and climbed up onto the edge of the boat. The captain was wearing bright yellow overalls, and the Steller caught him by the pants, pulled him over the side, and dragged him down. Stunned observers watched the yellow overalls get smaller and smaller as the sea lion pulled their owner deeper and deeper under the green water before finally letting him go.

A full-grown Steller bull had never even been caught — at least not alive. One group of fifteen men, all professional animal handlers, were out on a collecting trip. They were used to roping California sea lions, even big ones, and decided to try a Steller. They managed to get the heavy-duty lassoo around one enormous bull, and fifteen large, athletic humans braced themselves against the strain. Then the fifteen large, athletic humans were pulled off their feet like small children. The bull returned to the sea, taking the rope along with him — as a sort of souvenir, the handlers said.

There were some examples of Steller bulls being trained in captivity, though. At one point, I heard about a book that was supposed to tell how to train a Steller sea lion, and I got all excited and sent away for it. It turned out to be a small photo book showing how a giant Steller bull was trained from *outside* the pen. The trainer had a long pole and would lean over a wall and a deep moat full of water. Far below him, the Steller would obey a few simple commands such as "climb onto a rock."

This was how Stellers were usually handled. The technique was called "remote training." It worked kind of like the remote control on one of those radio-wave toy race cars, one that takes off at a distance from you as you hold the controls in your hand. That was how the trainers at Marine World had tried to train Cyrus, another Steller bull that had come to stay for a while several years earlier.

Nobody who ever saw Cyrus was likely to forget that half-ton giant. He was a typical Steller bull — magnificent to look at, but grouchy and aggressive.

Once, Cyrus had been bullying some yearling California sea lions, and handler Dee "Rags" Cross got worried. With the typical matter-of-fact courage of the animal handler, Rags went into the pen and started shooing the yearlings away, for their own safety. Cyrus watched for a moment and then got angry. He charged, slammed Rags up against the fence, and took the man's elbow in his mouth. He didn't bite down and break the bone. He just held the elbow joint in his mouth. One eye rolled up and looked at Rags, as if to say, "Do you know what I could do to you?" It was a long three minutes before Cyrus felt he had made his point and released the pressure on the handler's arm.

Cyrus had been moved to a different park, but his temperament hadn't changed. I had heard he was so strong he went through doors without bothering to open them first. A normal pen gate didn't even slow him down; he just chested his way right through it. A door bought from a human prison (it looked like a bank vault door) had to be installed in his pen at the new park. Now the high walls of his compound were solid concrete and reinforcing steel.

But in addition to these horror stories, there were also tantalizing hints that maybe, just maybe, if everything went right, a Steller bull could be trained to do a show. It would be a little like having your own *Tyrannosaurus rex* obeying your commands!

In a place called Harderwijk, in the Netherlands, a trainer named Ron Kastellaine and one of his assistants could go right into the pen of a full-grown Steller bull. They could actually touch the animal's mouth without losing fingers. Of course, Kastellaine's assistant had had the pup since birth. The animal had "imprinted" on him, giving him the emotional loyalty he would otherwise have given his mother.

There had also been an ace trainer named Roland Raffler, who had a contract with the Navy to train a partly grown, 625-pound Steller bull named Runner. (The Navy wanted to see if Stellers could be trained to track down sunken missiles.) Working at Point Mugu, California, Raffler had first concentrated on gentling the animal, who had been called "too mean to work with." He had succeeded, and I saw a photograph of the bull wearing a harness as he prepared to dive down and try to track a fallen missile. But there the story ended. The marine mammal center at Point Mugu was closed. Nobody knew how big the animal had gotten before his training was stopped, or where Raffler or Runner were now.

Given this kind of history, we didn't know what would happen with George and his training. But where there are challenges, there are also people who will rise to them. Sonny Allen, the head marine mammal trainer at our park, wanted to see how far he could go with a Steller bull. How thoroughly could he train this soon-to-be-giant animal before the inevitable occurred — before the fighting instincts took over in this lion of the sea?

5

Experiment in Training

When George was sixteen months old and scheduled to begin his formal training, he measured six feet from head to tail flippers and weighed 250 pounds. He certainly didn't look much like a baby anymore.

His dark, curly pup hair was gone, replaced by a smooth coat of cinnamon brown. He didn't have his gold mane yet, because he wasn't old enough. For him, the mane would be like whiskers on a teenage boy. But you could see where it would be. You could also tell he was going to be huge. When he put his front flippers on a fence and "stood up," George was as tall as a grown man, and heavier than most. But in Steller terms he was barely out of puphood. Ellie was almost as large, but her growth would slow down from now on. The size difference between them would become more noticeable day by day.

By now both George and Ellie lived entirely outdoors, as they would have in the wild. Their natural "sleeping bags" of muscle and blubber were thick enough to keep them warm even if they had slept on an iceberg.

In the Stellers' present open-roofed pen was a "training pedestal." This was a low, six-foot-long platform on short legs, with a smaller raised portion at one end for them to lean on. It had been with them from the beginning, and by now they had climbed back and forth over it so many times they knew there was no danger in the thing.

There was also a short pole with a round white ball on the end of it, which had been left leaning up against the outside of their fence, as if forgotten. The Styrofoam ball was actually a training "target." It had been left there so that the animals could investigate it from positions of safety. George had touched it with his whiskers, poking his nose through the fence mesh tentatively, ready to yank away if the thing tried to grab him. But it didn't. Since the target appeared to be neither capable of eating him nor edible itself, George soon left it alone.

But the target was important, and George and Ellie were about to find out why.

When the animals heard the familiar *clump, clump, clump* of boots approaching, they hurried to press their noses to the pieces of white plastic on the fence at the corner of the pen furthest from the gate. The clumping sound meant that food was coming. Experience had taught them that it would not be given to them until their noses were pressed against the plastic. The white squares were also targets. Teaching the pups to use them had been the beginning of their training.

The clumping boots belonged to Sonny Allen, the director of marine mammal training. A slender but muscular man, Sonny had the swiftness and grace of a martial artist, which, in fact, he was. He was a black belt in karate. Sonny had the ability to focus all his energies on whatever he did. He could really zero in on the animal he was training — an animal that could sometimes be partner, and sometimes opponent. When this expert trainer entered the pen, the rest of the world and its problems went away, and he gave the animal his complete concentration.

"Target, target . . . good boy, George; good girl, Ellie!" he said as the animals held their noses to the white plastic squares. "Okay," he said to his assistant, Frank Stryzalkowski, "if you'll work with Ellie over there, I'll work here with George."

Then he turned back to the young Steller male. "Okay, George, seat up, seat up — over here, that's right; follow the fish bucket up onto the training pedestal." *Wheeeet!* Sonny blew his whistle and rewarded George with a piece of fish.

This was George's first lesson in "seating up," which meant to climb up onto the training pedestal. His lower body was now on the platform, his chest resting against the high end. The pedestal was George's "school desk." Once he was there, it was time to learn.

"Okay, George, see this?" Sonny held up the white ball on the end of the stick. "This is a target, too. No, don't be scared. It can't hurt you. That's right — check it out. Uh-

huh, get those whiskers on it — target, target." The whistle blew again.

Because he was working with a Steller bull, Sonny had to start by trying to gentle George down. He began by making George hold his nose to the target while Sonny gently touched and patted him. He was showing George that there was no danger, always letting him know there was no reason to attack.

The first lesson (there would be four each day) was short and soon over. It may have looked easy to the average observer, but a lot of thought and effort and experience were behind it. The trainers had to find ways to bridge the huge gap between animal and human.

Imagine the difficulties for the sea lions! How could they figure out what the trainer wanted them to do? They are an entirely different species from humans. They obviously don't speak or understand our language. And during training, they're usually out of their natural element — water.

So how does a trainer communicate? Well, imagine that you're a student and I'm the teacher, and we're in a classroom together. We're just sitting there, and neither of us can say anything. After a while, your nose starts to itch, and you scratch it — and I give you a five-dollar bill. A couple of minutes later your nose itches again, and you scratch it again — and I give you another five-dollar bill. Once you figure out what I want, you'll probably start scratching your nose a whole lot! Similarly, if the animal does something right in training, it gets a reward. If it does something wrong, the trainer either says "No!" or says and does nothing.

At Marine World the whistle, food, and targets were the tools of animal training. Food had been the sea lion's first reward for doing what the trainer wanted. Then the whistle had been added, so that a "bridge" was established between the behavior and the food. Now the animals knew that a whistle sound meant a reward was coming.

The two kinds of targets served different purposes. The squares on the fence always stayed still. These were for the trainers' convenience. With the animals' noses pressed to the targets, the trainers could enter and leave the pen without the animals climbing all over them, looking for food. Touching the squares also signaled the beginning and end of training time. (Some more food at the end gave the animals something to look forward to.)

The moving target — the ball on the stick — was used to lead the animals through their show movements. For example, the target could be used to teach the beginning of a flip. The trainer would hold the target underwater and move it in a slow circle while the animal kept its nose pressed against it and followed. Or it could be used to get the animal swimming at top speed across the pool. The trainer would set the target up on the opposite side of the big training pool and point to it, saying, "Target!" and the animal would rocket across the pool.

Since training George was such an unusual challenge, Sonny Allen consulted with pinniped scientists like the renowned Dr. Ron Schusterman, who gave him much valuable information. Dr. Schusterman had done some fascinating work on communication with sea lions. (Some people thought it was even easier to communicate with sea lions than with dolphins.) With his assistant Kathy Krieger,

Dr. Schusterman had spent years teaching a simple sign language to the famous California sea lions Rocky and Bucky. Bucky could understand a whole complicated chain of hand signals. These might mean something such as "Fetch the large black square floating box over here." This actually required understanding several choices — "fetch" instead of "touch," and "square" instead of "round," for example. There was always a variety of objects in the pool, and the scientists sometimes worked with blindfolds on. That way, they could not subconsciously give the animals any clues as to what they were supposed to do.

One tip Dr. Schusterman gave Sonny about training George was to avoid teaching the behavior called "nodding." Nodding is very popular in shows featuring California sea lions. The up-and-down head signal means "yes" to most humans, and it can give the announcer something to make people laugh. "Do you think I'm good-looking?" the announcer might ask the animal. Then the trainer moves his fingers in the signal that means "nod," and the sea lion jerks its head up and down, as if it truly has an opinion on the subject.

But "yes" means "no" in Steller body language. When Steller bulls issue a warning to an opponent, they nod their heads, imitating the lunges they make when fighting. By rewarding them for nodding, a trainer might be encouraging them to become aggressive. So this time, Sonny didn't teach the nod. Also, he did a lot of work on "desensitizing" George's mouth. He tried to get George to allow his face and teeth to be touched without biting.

Over a period of months, Sonny taught George to walk on his front flippers. First, he had George lean across the training pedestal. After he leaned over, the trainer would touch George's back end. When George twitched his hind flippers, he got a reward of fish. Gradually he was rewarded for lifting his back end higher and higher, until all the weight was on his enormously powerful front flippers. (Strength was never a problem, and balance was not difficult for an athletic animal like George.) Pretty soon George could stand on his "hands." When that was achieved, the trainer walked away from George and called him. George flipper-walked to Sonny, appearing puzzled by all the delighted fuss that was made. He didn't refuse the reward of fish, however.

A favorite sea lion show maneuver, balancing a ball on the nose, was a little tough for George. California sea lions have a wide nose, which makes it fairly easy for them. But George's nose came to a sort of point. Sonny got around that by training George to flex his whiskers forward on command, giving the ball something to lean against!

Like anyone in school, George was often puzzled in training. He would look at Sonny for a moment, then twitch a flipper as if to say, "Is this what you want?" If he was right, the whistle would blow and the food would come. George liked that whistle a lot. But often he did not understand or would lose interest. Then the trainer had to find different ways to make the training fun and understandable.

Sonny was patient. He used small words and repeated a lot, always tying together a movement of his hands or body with a word signal. For example, when he wanted George to make his "ORR-ORR-ORR" noise so that people could hear what a Steller sounded like, he would hold his hand, palm up, and jerk the fingers toward his chest. He'd say, "Speak, George, speak . . . speak . . . speak." Every time he said it, his fingers would move. George would watch and watch, trying different things until he found the behavior that got him the fish. When he found it, he would usually do it again.

When George learned one behavior well, it would often be tied to another. This was called a "behavior chain." Teaching a flip, for example, involved several steps. As another Marine World trainer, Guenther "Gunner" Skamel, explains it, "You start with a leap, which you train by throwing a fish across the pool. The animal will dash for it, and when the animal comes back, it's moving at speed. You lift the target high out of the water, and as the animal leaps up to touch it, you turn the target in a circle and hope the animal follows. It usually doesn't. So then you put the target underwater and move it in a circle. The animal follows and gradually gets the idea of a circular motion."

How long does it take to make this happen?

"About three or four months, with a willing animal."

As the months passed, Sonny worked George up to a full twenty-eight behaviors, enough for an entire sea lion show. George's performance was captured on film, and the slides of the 450-pound Steller in action still exist today. Sometimes it seemed that George would prove to be the exception to the rule — that maybe he would grow and grow and still be controllable.

Sonny Allen was really a teacher, and he estimated that he had worked with approximately 300 sea lion "students." Even so, when I looked at George, I couldn't help feeling that, in a way, Sonny was a teacher in a very rough school.

George actually looked cute sometimes, but the wild was always there underneath.

Once I had watched a trained tiger get irritable. I was used to seeing the big striped cats act like oversized kittens. They bounded around so gracefully, and the trainers worked with them so smoothly, I thought that tigers were, well, sort of pussycats. But one day I was with a trainer beside a tiger pen, where he was feeding the tiger. He pushed a pan of meat through the feeding slot under the bars, and the tiger pounced on it, settled himself, and began to eat. "Watch this," the trainer said. *And then he touched the food tray.* That's all, just a finger touch. But the tiger's face changed, as if a mask had come off to show a monster underneath. The yellow eyes turned to blazing green, the facial muscles flexed and wrinkled, the lips drew back from the fangs. The tiger snarled in half-choked rage. Even on the safe side of the bars, I had a moment of stark terror. Then the peaceful face returned, and the tiger looked kittenish once again. But I never forgot that glimpse of the wild within.

George might be equally capable of turning to his wild side. I had seen photos of a bull Steller's skull, and the teeth were ugly and efficient. The smallest sea lion could do serious damage to a human, even by accident. One trainer was working with a sixty-pound yearling called Peabody, and an airplane flew over too low. Peabody got nervous and bit the nearest living thing, which happened to be the trainer's face. She needed some minor plastic surgery to prevent noticeable scarring, but she held no grudge against the animal. "It was an accident," she said. But still the teeth had cut her.

What could a larger animal do?

I had seen a 300-pound California sea lion take apart the redwood decking in his pen. He casually sank his teeth into the wooden two-by-fours, ripping them apart easily, like a one-sea-lion wrecking crew.

As for George, he kept on growing, getting bigger with each passing day. At full growth he might be twelve feet long and weigh 2,000 pounds or more. And with every inch and pound, the time grew closer when he would have to exert his will, testing himself and those who thought to control him.

6

The Sea Lion Who Said No

As George grew and his training progressed, he was brought from Seal Compound to Oceana Theatre. Here, he and Ellie could live in a backstage pen near the other performing sea lions. Also nearby were the killer whales in their tanks. At Oceana, George would have access to the 650,000-gallon main show pool, which was more fitting to his size than the smaller training pools. He and Ellie would train on Oceana's show stage and spend the rest of their time in their pen, with its individual pool and deck.

They were put together in the biggest of the pens, a few doors down from Nero. They could all see each other through the open-mesh fences. Funny thing, but Nero, the California sea lion who had "remodeled" my wetsuit, never gave George much trouble. They were kept apart, of course, and brought to the stage from different directions so they never had the chance to flat-out fight. But even so, Nero seemed to understand that he had better not hassle the increasingly huge Steller very much.

By this time I had made my peace with Nero. (Or rather, I had decided to forgive, if not forget, the time he had chomped on the south end of me.) One day I was watching trainer Patrick "Bucko" Turley work with Nero, and I asked him why he thought Nero had bitten me.

"We think Nero may have been abused when he was younger," Bucko said. "Early trainers used to beat sea lions with sticks if they wouldn't learn. That might have happened to Nero, because even now he'll freak at the sight of anything that looks like a stick. If a janitor walks by with a broom, Nero will run for the water as fast as he can. And if you're in his way, he might inflict a substantial bite on you." I thought about the scrub brush I had taken with me into Nero's territory. Maybe he had also been acting out a territorial urge to protect his home against intruders.

Nero had a sort of general all-purpose bark to announce his possession of his territory. He also had a more serious challenging bark, but that one he kept to himself, or used only on smaller California sea lions — never on George.

George never barked at all. Like all Stellers, he "spoke" less often, but when he did, it meant more. If he wanted to make noise, he definitely could. His voice was powerful, elemental — like an earthquake or a storm. His growls had variety, ranging from deep to deeper, right down to a basement grumble. He would give a pulsing roar sometimes as he paced across the stage, an "ORR-ORR-ORR-ORR," like an outboard motor starting up. Or he might emit a long, slow belch, the kind a rowdy human would make, but with infinitely more depth and feeling. He could let out or take in his breath in a loud, long hiss. And even as a bull he would still make a noise like "Ahh?" if startled, as he had done when a pup.

But when he was frustrated — when he couldn't understand what the trainers wanted or was not allowed to have his way — then George would throw back his head and let out his full-fledged challenge roar. When he cut loose with that, it was as if the earth shook.

Sonny Allen sometimes put on scuba tanks and went swimming with George in the main pool. No human can keep up with a Steller in the water, but as Sonny swam, George would hurtle away and then whip back near to him. There was an underwater viewing window beneath the stage at Oceana, and I loved to look through and watch the way human and animal enjoyed each other's company in the water. At such moments, it seemed as if Sonny and George could go on having fun forever, like a couple of happy kids.

At this point, George was about six years old and was going through what in humans would be called puberty, the time when a person turns from a child into a young adult. For George, this meant that he was not only getting ready for mating, but also for the inevitable fighting a bull must do to earn the right to reproduce.

At 650 pounds, George was full of energy! With no other bulls to wrestle, he wanted to practice his roughhousing with Eleanor. Sometimes the two of them could make an incredible commotion.

Once, George got so worked up that he broke the decking in his pen. The deck was a heavy square of wood, wedged into slots in the concrete wall. George got so active that he actually bent the wood and forced it out of the slots. He was like an oversized kid who won't stop jumping on the bed until he breaks it. I had to go in and hoist the thick structure back up, then pound some brackets into the wall as further support for the deck. You can be sure I did the work when George was in the next pen over.

George could be rough on his "toys," too. He had a huge old empty metal beer barrel that he liked to bang around, and the massive dents on it were impressive reminders of his strength.

He had astonishing endurance as well as strength. Sometimes when I was cleaning the pen next to his, I would watch him underwater. He would start swimming in his little pool, which was only about twenty-five feet long. This wasn't much for an animal his size, but he would give a great yank of his flippers, which sent him rocketing toward the wall. Just before he crashed, he would flip-turn, shoot back, and rip toward the wall at the other end of the pool. Then he'd flip again, over and over, until the water looked like a foaming white wheel, and the waves leaped onto the walkway above. He would keep up this strange race-and-turn in the small quarters of his pool for hours on end.

Once, while I was watching him underwater from the next pen over, he turned and roared at me. I couldn't hear the noise through my wetsuit's rubber hood. But I saw the bubbles come out of his mouth, and I *felt* the sound vibrating through my chest.

I hadn't the slightest urge to imitate Sonny and go swimming with George.

Once George came of age reproductively, he bothered Ellie no end whenever the spring mating season arrived. Like all female Stellers, Ellie would mate once a year, and once only. Like all bulls, George wanted to mate as often as possible. Ellie did allow George to mate once with her. But after that, she would only hiss at him, or discourage him with a bite. Once she even gave George a bloody nose, but nothing stopped him for long.

When George got to be too much hassle for poor Ellie, the trainers would put her in the next pen over, to give her a rest. They hated to do this, because, hassles or not, both animals appeared to enjoy each other's company.

Even though George still had his good moments, there were more and more signs that his training was starting to break down.

One of the big problems was time. Sonny did not have enough hours in the day to concentrate on George. His job as director of marine mammal training meant that he was responsible for a parkful of animals — dolphins, killer whales, seals, and the other sea lions, as well as George. And as a director he had endless meetings to attend, forms to fill out, letters to answer — all kinds of paperwork. Although George also trained with Bucko Turley and Frank Stryzalkowski, his real attachment was to Sonny.

These days George would indeed shuffle through an increasing series of behaviors. In one, he would raise his flipper to his head in what could stand for a "salute," "prayers," or pretend embarrassment. But his real emotions were perhaps more accurately judged by his bulging eyes and shortened breath, and by the way he would walk directly toward the trainer, closer and closer, trying to deny the trainer any territory of his own.

As Bucko later put it, "Ellie never did get really out of hand. But George, well, as George got bigger, he was constantly pushing his weight around, posturing, showing off, sticking his chest out and shoving, chasing the other animals around. He always had to be in control, like putting his head on top of Ellie's head, and shoving her down. He had endless energy, too. And a fantastic appetite — twenty pounds of fish, morning and night."

Until now the trainers' height had been sufficient to intimidate George; in the wild, he would have fled from an animal bigger than himself. But now, even on all fours, he was almost as tall as the three main trainers, Sonny, Bucko, and Frank. And when George put his front flippers up onto something like a fence or a training pedestal, his head was now higher than theirs. In the wild, the bigger animals are usually in charge.

Increasingly George looked at his trainers in a new way. It was as if he were thinking, "You were bigger than me once; but you're not now. You were in charge back then, but now I'm a bull, and why should I obey you?"

As George's natural aggression displayed itself more and more, the training sessions became wars of will. He would make sudden charges toward the trainer, and then turn away as if he had only been joking. The trainers' domination took more and more effort to achieve; the cooperation for which they strived was offered less and less.

As I watched events develop, I saw drama in the increasing tension between trainer and animal. It was like a movie in which you know a fight is going to happen, but you aren't sure when.

Trainers see things differently. To Sonny, working with an animal who was able to physically ruin him was just a risk to be accepted, like the possibility of an industrial injury in a factory. Later, I tried several times to get Sonny to talk to me about it, to tell what it was like when George began to get out of control. But the trainer would only shrug and say, "I could see that the training was getting to be no fun for him."

The end, when it came, happened in a manner completely unexpected.

Sonny Allen had to go to Japan, to deliver a killer whale named Kianu to a new oceanarium there. He would be gone for four months. No one knew for sure, of course, how George felt about losing the trainer to whom he was closest. But I suspect he felt a little like a dog in the pound, one that has been shuffled among too many homes and has now decided he trusts nobody. Or maybe the timing just happened to coincide with George's growing too big and aggressive.

Time had passed. George was now six years old. In the shadows behind the pen door his bulk loomed large and indistinct.

One day Bucko arrived as usual for a training session. "Okay, George, let's go," he said. Sullenly George shuffled toward the white plastic panel set in the mesh fence, as he always did before coming out. But he only put his nose halfway to it, and he let out a low, grumbling roar as he did.

The gate swung back.

Eight hundred pounds of Steller sea lion emerged. Slowly, swaying his great head, neck, and shoulders exaggeratedly from side to side, George moved step by unhurried step across the backstage floor of Oceana Theatre. He paused beside old Nero's pen and snorted at Nero. Nero only dived into his pool, seeming to remember some business he had to attend to in the water beneath the floorboards.

With Bucko's urging, George finally reached the Oceana stage.

"Okay, George, seat up!" said Bucko. George looked away as if he had not heard, or as if nothing worth hearing had been said. He made a low, rumbling mutter.

"Seat up, George!" repeated Bucko, putting more authority into his voice. There was a training session to be done.

George put one flipper up on the pedestal, but added no weight to it. He was barely touching the pedestal just to see how little he could do and still get a fish.

"No, George," said Bucko firmly. He was not going to reward George for nearly disobeying him.

The Steller pulled his flipper back, turned, and looked at Bucko.

"Seat up, George," continued Bucko. "Seat up!"

For a moment George paused, as if torn between obeying the trainer and attacking him. Suddenly he made his move. With a lurch and shuffle he exploded into motion, coming straight at Bucko — and past him, diving into one of the side holding pools.

He snorted out air as he dived into the pool, and there was an answering exhalation of steam, and a sudden swirl of motion.

The pool into which George had jumped was already occupied. A fourteen-foot, 5,000-pound female killer whale named Vigga had been swimming peacefully around her tank. Vigga was of the type of killer whale that hunts seals, sea lions, and even other whales. These huge creatures can knock out even the biggest sea lion bull with one blow of the tail. Killer whales were never put into the main pool when the sea lions were there; they stayed in their holding pools. When Vigga saw a sea lion in her holding pool, nobody had to tell her what to do. In a flash of black and white, she turned and came at the "food" that had just dropped in.

As two and a half tons of killer whale hurtled across the pool at George, he seemed to realize he had just made a serious mistake. Changing directions so fast it seemed he almost left skid marks, George raced for the side of the pool, making tremendous front-flipper pulls. He reached the edge of the tank with the killer whale right behind him. George yanked his big body out of the water, leaped onto the stage, and was back up on that training pedestal so fast he almost knocked it over. Vigga slid halfway up on the stage on her side, reaching with that safe-door mouth wide open, pink throat and white teeth showing, as she did when she wished to be fed. Anyone who has seen killer whales snatching seals off the beach would have known precisely what she had in mind.

There was no more trouble with George that particular afternoon. He stayed right on the pedestal and behaved himself, with no more than an occasional glance at the water where the killer whale swam.

Even so, it was an ending.

Sonny Allen called from Japan almost daily, to see how things were going. When Bucko told the head trainer what George had done, Sonny sighed and told Bucko to discontinue the training.

When Sonny returned, he worked with George a couple more times. George was plainly glad to see him, swimming in tight circles and eagerly clambering onto the training pedestal.

But all too soon the grumbling began again, and the challenges. Although he didn't become violent or attack the trainers, he was balky and uncooperative. Sometimes George would work, and sometimes he wouldn't. Show sea lions have to be reliable, and increasingly George was not. His show behaviors were sometimes sloppy and half-done.

From now on, the problem would get worse. If a sea lion says no to its trainers, there isn't much the trainers can do about it. They can hold back on food for a few minutes, or turn and walk away, letting the animal know it did something wrong — but that's about all. Starvation tactics or beatings are not only loathsomely cruel but also ineffective. Sea lions retain their wildness. If treated cruelly, they may simply turn off to food and to life itself, preferring death to domination. Trainers work hard for cooperation, but if for reasons of its own the sea lion will not be part of a show, then the training must end.

Now we were left with a serious problem. What were we going to do with George? For the moment, he and Ellie were transferred back to Seal Compound, where they had begun. (Where George went, Ellie went, too.) And there, oddly enough, a killer whale's cousin brought me face-to-face with George.

7

Face to Face with
"Big Baby"

Danger often comes in unexpected ways. Before I went to work at Marine World, I would never have thought that dolphins would harm humans, even though they *are* cousins to the killer whale. But then, no wild animal likes to be caught and held still against its will. And that was what I had to do one afternoon to a dolphin named Ernestine, in the dolphin training tank.

Ernestine was sleek and swift and beautiful. Normally we were friends, but that day I had been trying to catch her underwater. Wearing wetsuit, mask, fins, and snorkel tube, I was facedown on the surface, studying her gray body as she whipped back and forth in one narrow area of the tank. We had stretched a net across part of the tank, to cut down the dolphin's swimming room. But there was still plenty of space for escape and evasion, and she was very much in command. We didn't want to just scoop her up with the nets, because the knots where the cords joined might hurt her delicate hide.

I was trying to get Ernestine out of the water so that the vet could take a routine blood sample. In later years, dolphins would be trained to swim over to the side of the tank and cooperate with the vet. But back then, a diver like me had to swim out and put a sort of aquatic tackle on the animal. Sometimes the grab worked; sometimes it didn't. If the dolphin wanted to fight back or get away, it very definitely had the strength and speed to do so.

Usually, by watching Ernestine, I could see the exact moment when she was ready to give up. She would then allow me or one of the other divers to gently take hold and guide her to the side of the tank. There we would put her carefully into a canvas stretcher and lift her out of the tank. She could be back in the water in less than five minutes. But that day it was not so simple.

Ernestine did not want to be caught, and she let me know it in the clearest way she could. Her open jaws slashed from side to side, then snapped together, as she nodded her head up and down (as with a Steller, this yes motion indicates anger). She made her serious threat noise — *klonk!* — and dashed rapidly back and forth, warning me in every way short of a phone call *not* to mess with her.

It was good advice, and I should have listened. I could have backed off for a while, taken a ten-minute break, and then come back to see if she had changed her mind. Frequently this worked. But foolish pride overcame my common sense; I didn't want to look afraid. Ignoring her warnings, I came ahead anyway.

With my body just beneath the surface, I came toward her. I was crowding her, keeping the pressure on, making repeated unsuccessful grabs. I could tell this was making her angrier, but I didn't know what else to do.

Then I thought I had her. Like a coiled spring, she was down at the bottom, where the net came together with the wall. She snapped her jaws one more time. I took a deep breath to swim down and get her, when Ernestine stopped warning. She came at me, fast, in a way I'd never seen before.

Shooting straight toward me as if she were going to ram me, the dolphin changed direction at the last minute in a sort of forward roll. Her tail came across and *slammed* the side of my head. The impact was stunning, knocking me back and upward, half my body's length into the air.

As I sank back down, I heard a buzzing *seeseeseesee* as the water entered my left eardrum, which had burst with the force of the blow. I felt dizzy and sick. When I pulled myself out of the water, the ground seemed to swirl around me. I had to reach back to the edge of the tank, holding on tight, to make the world stay still.

There was something wrong inside my head. My balance was way off. Now, any diver who gets hit in the head will automatically try to "clear" by pinching the nose and blowing out those inner passages in the head called the eustachian tubes. This makes a clicking sound and bulges out the eardrums slightly. But not that day. That day when I pinched my nose and blew, I heard a hiss as the air came out through the hole in my left eardrum. If I had been a smoker, which of course I was not, I could have blown smoke out my left ear.

"Six weeks," the doctor said — a whole month and a half before I could dive again. I would have to stay out of the water, working "dry" until my eardrum scarred over.

What would I do at the park in the meantime?

"Work in the cut shack," management answered. "You can help John Benner prepare the seal and sea lion food and take care of the animals."

It was six o'clock on a chilly morning when I reported for my first day on the new and temporary job. As I opened the gray door to the cut shack, or food preparation room, I saw that John Benner was there ahead of me. Originally from the Pacific island of Guam, J.B. was a huge man — 230 pounds, heavily muscled, and extremely strong. Yet he was so gentle and soft-spoken that there was no threat about him — no hint of the intimidation that large men some-times convey.

J.B. was special — one of those heroes of hard work who quietly makes the world a better place. He was technically in a management position, so he didn't get overtime pay if he worked a seventy-hour week, which he often did. As everyone knew, he would go to any length to protect his "babies" — the seals and sea lions in his care.

Once, when a mother seal died, J.B. slept all night in a wet wooden travel cage. Why? Because of the baby. The pup was deprived of its mother for the first time in its short life, and it had been whining and calling out. J.B. was worried. "He might be cold," he said, "and lonely, too!" A heat lamp shone into the pen, which was kept in Sonny Allen's office, and the baby really would have been all right. But in the morning we found J.B. curled up, shivering, with the seal pup snug in the circle of his arms.

I always felt that J.B. moved in a sort of self-created Eden where everything and everyone around him seemed affected by his attitude. Both humans and animals were gentler — on their best behavior — when J.B. was around.

Right then J.B. was bending over one of the eight stainless-steel sinks, with bare arms stuck deep in the gray water. He smiled and nodded good morning, but he never stopped his work. As he lifted a handful of something out of the water, I noticed his hands were purplish red. I looked in the sink and understood why. Around floating plastic packs of fish and squid were half-thawed chunks of ice.

The night before, boxes and boxes of frozen squid and fish had been taken out of the walk-in freezer at the back of the cut shack. This was all high-quality food, like what you see in the freezer section of the supermarket. The boxes had been emptied and the plastic-wrapped blocks of food set in sinks full of water. Then the faucets were adjusted so that a trickle of water flowed over the food all night and thawed it slowly. (If it thawed too quickly, it got mushy, and the animals wouldn't touch it.)

Now I joined J.B. at the sinks and tore the plastic packs apart, flinging the wrappers happily behind me. (It's kind of fun to make a mess, even if you are the one who will have to clean it up!) Then I scooped a handful of round, pink-fleshed Vietnamese squid onto the sink's cutting board.

Each squid had to be depenned. A squid doesn't have a

backbone, but in the center of its body is a clear, thin, sturdy "pen," which looks like an old-fashioned quill pen, the kind made from bird feathers. This pen is stiff and sharp, and we had to take it out because it might scratch our animals' throats.

The squid came in sacks of fifty each, and I had to depen twenty sacks. I pushed on the tentacles, and the head and large dark eye separated from the insides. It sounds gross but it wasn't. Well, not *too* gross, anyway. I flicked the squid pen off the cutting board.

I had just depenned one squid. Only 999 more left to do.

I finished the sinkful as fast as I could — which is to say, rather slowly. J.B. zipped through his. Then he went on to "pill" the thawed mackerel, inserting chalky-blue vitamin tablets through each fish's red gills into the body cavity, three or four pills to the fish. He laid this special food on top of already partly filled buckets, each labeled with the name of an animal — Coco, Patches, George, Mother, Lou — in black letters on the side. J.B. weighed the buckets so that he'd know exactly how much was eaten by whom. Later he would record the information in a notebook that the vets would read. If an animal ate less or more than usual, this told the vet something about its health.

"Okay, let's go feed Seal Compound," said J.B., lugging two silver buckets out to the waiting electric cart. "If this thing starts," he added. It did. With a quiet click, the electric cart started up. Although its battery system always seemed to need fixing, the cart was a quiet, pollution-free way to haul forty-pound buckets of fish to the animal pens.

Seal Compound, a roomy corner of the park surrounded and subdivided by open-mesh fencing, was home to several species of water mammals. There were harbor seals, Asian river otters, several yearling sea lions, and two elephant seals, in addition to George and Ellie.

The animals shared a large, shallow pool in the compound. As J.B. and I entered, I noticed that in the middle of the pool was — a nose. All I could see were two nostrils that looked as big as twin snorkel tubes when the animal breathed and the nostrils flexed open. The nose moved, and I caught a glimpse of a huge, sleek head. The outline and size of the body underneath were hidden by the murky, roiled water, but I couldn't help noticing that each of the eyes looked as big as a fist.

Then my attention was distracted. Before me now was one of the biggest, and without question the *ugliest,* creatures I had ever seen.

First of all, Mother, the park's female elephant seal, was a trifle on the heavy side, weighing roughly 3,000 pounds. Also, there was stuff coming out of her nose. Strands of yellow mucus thick as noodles hung down and shook back and forth when she moved. I had the urge to get a handkerchief and wipe her nose for her. But I would have needed a whole blanket. And her nose was actually small compared to that of the nearby male sea elephant called Lou. His bulbous snout was so big that noises echoed in it when he called for food, as he did now — "UNK-UNK-UNK-UNK!" Both animals were molting, losing last year's coats in rags and tatters, as was natural for them. There was good new hide underneath, but right now they looked awful.

Then J.B. said, "Hello, Mother," and smiled at the big elephant seal like family. I felt faintly ashamed, for he apparently saw something lovable, though I could not.

Mother leaned her head back and opened her mouth, which looked as wide as the hole under a manhole cover. J.B. dropped a couple of mackerel down the cavernous open throat. Then he seemed to remember something.

"You keep feeding Mother," he said. "I'll be right back," he added, more to Mother than to me, and clumped off in his white rubber boots.

Mother arched backward so far that the top of her head almost touched her tail. Despite her enormous bulk, she was astonishingly flexible. Then she belched, and it sounded like a giant with indigestion. Was this a sign of irritation? Was she getting mad?

"Oh, right, sorry, Mother."

I had forgotten that I was supposed to be feeding her. Let's see, how had J.B. done it? Pinching thumb and forefinger around a blue-skinned mackerel, I held it over the wide pink mouth and let go. The mackerel dropped between the huge teeth, falling cleanly down the throat, not even touching the sides. I could have sworn I heard a splash as the fish landed in Mother's stomach.

Mother moved — not an easy thing for her. Elephant seals do not saunter casually. The movement began as a slow, rippling bulge near her tail that advanced through her blubber like a wave in a waterbed, until the ripple reached her upper body and head, lifting her slightly. As her front end came up off the ground, her back end came forward as well, landing with a *shhhlumping* thud, after which she paused to rest. She had gained perhaps six inches. *Shhhlump*.

Another half-foot of progress. I almost panted with her, the effort was so obvious.

"AAORRRRR!" An enormous shadow covered mine. I heard a strange hissing noise, the scrape of wet hair and hide touching concrete at high speed. I caught a glimpse of something huge and red-brown erupting from the pool, but I did not pause to identify it.

I am normally slow-moving, but I make exceptions in moments of terror. There was a ten-foot chain-link fence in my way. I believe I touched it on the way over, but I cannot be sure. When I was conscious of the roaring again, I was on the opposite side of the fencing. Only then did I pause and turn to look.

And there was George, who now weighed roughly 1,000 pounds, standing on the concrete by the fish bucket.

The Steller sea lion was huge but athletic-looking — nothing like the clumsy elephant seal. Eyes rimmed with a startling ring of white caught mine. And muscles? This animal looked like a pro-football linebacker, massive but agile, swift, and totally in command. He vocalized again, but softer and lower now, with a slow, guttural, "orrrrr, orrrrr, orrrrr."

Then the great head shot down, and the jaws buried themselves in the forty-pound bucket of mackerel I had abandoned. As George's enormous front flippers adjusted the container, muscles rippled in his shiny, gold-flecked back.

Mother made a noise at the theft of her food, but it was apparently too much trouble to do anything but complain.

Then, to my astonishment, I heard, "George, you bad boy!" J.B. was back beside me, frowning at George through the fence. J.B. had to make a real effort to show disapproval.

But George had known J.B. since his first day at Marine World and looked on him almost as he would a mother. The huge Steller bull acted like a kid caught with his hand in the cookie jar. George hurled himself back into the pool, hitting the water so hard that waves crashed up and over onto the surrounding concrete. Presently the big head appeared above the water again, though it ducked under to the nostrils while J.B. was scolding.

"Don't let him bully you," said J.B. as I clambered awkwardly back over the fence I had so lightly cleared a moment before. J.B. looked at me in a puzzled way, but he was too polite to ask why I was climbing back over the fence. He just walked to the pen's gate, opened it, and went in. I jumped down from the fence to the concrete inside the animals' pen. Well, yes, I did realize that people normally used the gate to go in and out of a pen, but . . .

"He's only a big baby," said J.B. "Don't let him steal Mother's food."

"Big Baby" leered at me from behind J.B.'s back.

"You shake your broom at him if he tries to take Mother's food again — but don't hurt him!" he added hastily.

I promised not to hurt the poor, helpless creature.

"Now come help me feed the otters and scrub out their pen." And we went through a gate into the adjoining otter pen.

Otters! What a delight these water mammals were. Brown-furred and bright-eyed, they were in constant motion, always looking for fun.

Their little paws plucked at the edges of my pants leg

and the laces of my work boot. As one otter pulled a pants cuff out of my boot, I sat down for a minute to play, or rather to be played with. The otter climbed right up my chest and onto my shoulders, as if we'd known each other always. He sniffed inquisitively in my ear and rummaged through the roots of my hair, in case there was something valuable in there.

I felt like hugging him, but of course I didn't. He was no toy. Once I had tried to pet an otter while it was eating, and it had turned instantly fierce, its nose and lips curling back from its white fangs. So now, I just sat still and enjoyed this otter's nearness.

"Clean their floor real well, okay?" J.B. told me. Then he rushed off to bring food and affection to the animals in another pen.

A heavy black hose that hung over the fence between the otter pen and the main compound shot clean water onto the pen's concrete floor. This hose (or rather its location) was about to become important to me.

With my broom, I scrubbed up the manure, and the water sluiced the mess away, chasing it down a concrete channel which led out to a drain. I called to J.B. to turn off the water. Nobody answered except a seagull settling on the fence.

"J.B.?" I called again. My eyes followed the path of the black hose, over the fence, along the floor — right past the pool occupied by George. The faucet was inside the compound, next to the pool. One hundred feet, not more. All I had to do was to open one gate, walk past George, and turn off the water. That was all. Few opportunities have appealed to me less.

I saw a small ripple in the center of the pool, as if George was shifting position under the water.

Water kept on gushing from the black hose. Might as well get a drink, I thought. But the pressure was too great, and the water bounced out of my mouth before I could swallow very much.

J.B.! There he was now, in the electric cart. He was coming to rescue me! The need for personal courage slipped away. J.B. would saunter into the compound, and I would casually enter from the otter pen and follow him out. Nobody would know how George had made me feel.

But the electric cart drove over the bridge into the main park, and was gone.

J.B.! I thought. I guess you got to thinking about your animals, and your human friend slipped your mind completely!

The water continued to flow. I considered my choices. The only gate to the otter pen led back into the compound. I could leave the water running, climb out the back way over the otter pen's fence, and forget it until next feeding time. Or I could climb out the back way, go around the whole compound, and poke my fingers or a stick through the open mesh and turn the faucet off in safety.

From the pool George lifted his head and made an impolite noise in my direction. I felt my lower lip start to stick out, the way it used to when I was a kid and felt like defying my mother. I picked up the broom and gave it a shake. My stomach also gave a little shake as I opened the gate to the main compound.

"ORRRR!" George boomed at me, leaping up onto the pool's edge.

I answered him, shouting, "HEYYYY!" and charging toward him. The head of the broom slammed into George's belly. The giant sea lion fell back and disappeared in a welter of foam. I couldn't believe it. It had been so simple.

I turned off the water with a flourish, and stalked in elbow-swinging pride past the pool where my former terror lay hiding. Hmmf, guess I showed him a thing or two, I thought. But I was congratulating myself a little prematurely.

"AOURRRR!" he roared, towering over me again. His jaws were opened wide, and the giant brown teeth showed clearly. I smelled his fishy breath. My body went hot and cold all over.

I waved my broom like crazy and shook it so hard in front of him that, suddenly, the bristle-block end of the broom flew off!

George and I watched the long brush head soar through the air, turning end over end and landing *clunkflopflop* on the opposite side of the pool. Oh my, I thought, I have just lost my defenses.

But if the flying broom head startled me, it astonished George. This had never happened before! His huge form whirled and in one motion heaved itself into the pool. The water boiled with little harbor seals flung out of the way of the bull's mad rush.

I hollered after him, hoping he would think it was me he had been frightened of, and not the flying broom head.

"And you remember that!" I shouted at his nose, when it emerged again from the middle of the pool.

Then the rush of adrenaline slowed, and my knees began

to shake again. I tried to strut as I left the compound, but I'm not sure I was entirely convincing.

To a professional animal handler or trainer, controlling big animals was part of everyday life. A story like that of George and the broom was just talk for lunchtime, something mumbled round a mouthful of sandwich, then forgotten. For me, tricking a half-ton Steller with a broom was an incident to remember. But in practical terms, it meant only that I was fit to feed him, that I could carry his food buckets without having to run.

During the next month and a half, I had to shake my broom at George about five or six times. Although I was impressed and fascinated by him, I never was able to relax around him. I had neither the techniques of the trainers nor a long association, like that of J.B., to fall back on in my dealings with George.

It was a little frightening just to watch George play with his food. He would take a blue mackerel almost two feet long and shake it in half with his teeth. Or he might toss it twenty feet in the air with an agile flip of his enormous neck. It wasn't hard to imagine what could happen if those teeth took hold of you. For that matter, he was getting so big that he wouldn't even have to bite. He could just run over a person and squash him or her with his bulk.

Although he had never harmed anybody, it was clear that the people around George couldn't always maintain complete control over him. And he was still growing; he could get to be *twice* as big as he was now.

What were we going to do with him?

8

The Problem Grows Bigger

*A*t first it was funny when George figured out how to work the latch on the gate to his pen adjoining Seal Compound. Using his teeth, the Steller simply lifted the sliding metal gate lock out of its seat and let himself out for a walk. He was spotted immediately, of course — a thousand-pound sea lion is not hard to notice — and lured back to his pen with some mackerel.

The gate was padlocked, and we thought that was the end of it.

But then George discovered what Cyrus before him had known — that is, how much fun it is to go through gates without opening them.

Like all of his kind, George was pushy, a leaner. Even as a pup he had liked to push up against the handler's legs, shoving him back a foot or two at a time. "You'd take a step back, and he would take that space, and keep coming," handler Ed Comer recalled. "Before you knew it, you'd be way over someplace else from where you had started."

Now that George was getting really big, his shoving tendencies increased. They began to take the form of a slide-and-slam. With a quick running start he would work up speed and then dive forward on his chest, holding head and flippers back. He would slide swiftly across the hard, smooth concrete — and slam into the fence. He bent the fence, jamming the mesh so that it stayed permanently arched with the bulging outline of his body.

Next, he broke the gate, padlock and all. The metal gate poles bent and separated across his massive chest. The cheap padlock exploded, and the sliding latch would not slide anymore.

We got a new and more expensive padlock, new poles, and a new latch — and tied the gate bars together with a double coil of heavy bike chain. The chain and lock finally stopped him from going through. Although he still kept bending the fence until the whole lower half was permanently warped, everybody breathed a sigh of relief.

Until George remembered that Stellers can climb.

It started with a six-foot fence. Now that George was living at Seal Compound again, he spent part of his time in the large compound pool and part in his own smaller pen. Next to his pen was Ellie's. The fence George chose to climb was the one between his and Ellie's pens.

"Didn't we pen them apart?" the handlers asked one morning, as George raised his head from its resting place on Ellie's back. He looked so innocent.

"I thought so — come on, George, in your house!" George calmly followed the food bribe, galumphing into his own pen, *flipflopflipflop* — until the trainers left. As soon as they were out of sight, big George reached his flippers up onto the fence and pulled himself over again. The move was perfectly smooth and easy, as if he had practiced it — which he undoubtedly had.

The handlers did not want the two animals together. George was just too rough with Ellie. His energies were intended for a larger stage than this. In the wild he would have had great distances to swim, and there would have been other Steller bulls for him to fight. Here, all he had to focus his power on was comparatively small Ellie. He was not being a bully — he was just being a bull.

Sometimes George seemed to get jealous over Ellie. One day, from his pen, he spotted Ellie having some innocent fun. She was zipping back and forth with the yearling California sea lions in the large compound pool. The California sea lion yearlings were not interested in Ellie romantically. They were mere "babies" who weighed only forty pounds apiece, roughly what George had weighed the day he was born.

But George stood up, roaring, and pulled himself over the fence with one tug of his flippers. After landing on his chest with a loud thump, he got up instantly and charged. The yearlings fled in terror, dashing off in all directions at once. Ellie zipped out of the pool. George cornered her, roaring first at her and then at the yearlings. His eyes did

something quite peculiar. One eye stared right at Ellie, while the other eye rolled fiercely around in its socket, trying to keep track of everybody else. In the wild, this ability allowed one eye to watch something in detail while the other eye kept track of the big picture, alert for any strange or sudden movement.

Once he learned how, George kept on climbing. One night he scared a night watchman half out of his wits. The man, new to the park, saw something stirring in the shadows of George's pen and turned his flashlight on it.

It was George, of course. The huge creature charged, hit the fence, and came over it, as the poor night watchman ran for his life. He didn't know that George was not trying to catch him. Like the mountain gorillas of Africa, who thump their chests and chase intruders only to the edge of their territory, George was just chasing the invader away. Having routed the man from his turf, George calmly climbed back into his pen.

At about this time, trainer Pete Cobb had an even scarier encounter with George. The trainers had worked hard from the beginning to keep George from becoming "mouthy," or dangerous with his teeth. Most training sessions had included desensitizing time, when the trainers stroked or patted George on the neck, shoulders, and face, and rewarded him for not biting them. This was important because if George was too sensitive about being touched and reacted with a bite, he could crush a human's bones. Although Stellers have never been known to attack humans, the decision to bite or not remains with the creature who owns the teeth.

We were reminded of this one hot summer day when

Pete went in to feed George. There was no water in the compound's main pool. The asphalt was being repainted, and the pool could not be refilled until the paint was dry. George was hot and miserable. He wanted to get into some nice, cool water, and the bathtub in his pen was too small for him now.

So, when Pete came into the pen that day, George was in a foul mood. He controlled his temper until he ate the fish Pete brought. But when the fish ran out, leaving George still a bit hungry, the animal roared and came at the trainer. Pete stood up straight to face him, standing as tall and calm as he could. But even on all fours George was now so big he could almost look the man in the eye.

George slammed Pete up against the wall of the pen. For a moment Pete was looking straight into George's red eyes. Then the sea lion whipped his head down to Pete's knee and put his jaws around it. Pete could feel the sharp edges of teeth toying with his kneecap. If he bit down . . .

One of George's eyes studied Pete's face; the other eye took in the rest of the pen, in case anyone else wanted trouble. Then abruptly the animal let go and turned away, allowing Pete to hobble to safety. No permanent damage had been done, but the threat was clear.

After this and other similar incidents, those concerned with George began a serious review of their options. One suggestion was to set George up in Seal Cove, one of the most beautiful exhibits in the park. Seal Cove was a natural-looking re-creation of a sea lion rookery. The half-mile stretch of lagoon was connected to the open water of the nearby bay and surrounded by a fence to keep the animals in.

A log wall topped with planter boxes hid the Seal Cove gate. Behind it was a concrete slide-out area and an open expanse of water dotted with man-made islands. There lived fourteen harbor seals and California sea lions.

I remember one day when Gunner Skamel, his assistant Bill Winhall, and I went to feed the animals in Seal Cove. Bill drove an old electric cart, its flat bed sagging under shining buckets of herring, blue mackerel, and squid. The animals were ready and eager. They knew very well what the silver buckets meant. They had been forewarned by the seagulls that food was on the way.

We lifted down the buckets, opened the gate, stepped inside — and the sea lions came. This was their second feeding, and they would eat again this evening. But you would never have known it from the way the horde rushed toward us. Muscular brown bodies, glistening with water, heaved themselves onto the concrete slope.

We hustled out fish as fast as we could, but even then it was a struggle not to be overrun. Massive sea lion bulls, slender females, pups, and leopard-spotted harbor seals — all were determined to get their fair (or unfair) share. Often a mackerel thrown to one small harbor seal was intercepted by a lunging sea lion bull. Bill and Gunner called out names, locating the shy ones, and keeping track to make sure everybody got enough. Gray and white seagulls massed and screamed nonstop overhead, diving when they saw a chance to snatch a fish.

"That's Alex, the dominant bull in Seal Cove now," explained Bill. "It's easy to tell, 'cause the dominant ones come in the closest and make the most noise."

But one huge bull sat apart from the rest, eyes closed,

nose high, making neither move nor gesture toward the food. Gunner tossed a mackerel very gently to him, almost laying it before him. As the fish splashed into the water, the animal bent down and poked around for a few seconds, then straightened and swallowed. Then he sat still again, eyes closed, seeming not to care whether or not more food came.

"That's Renegade," said Gunner, his face turning serious. "He was the dominant bull until he got bitten in the face by Alex, in one of the territorial fights they have. Mostly they don't tear each other up too much, but this time Renegade got bitten across the eyes. The vets medicated him as best they could, but we think he's blind."

These bulls were big — 600, maybe as much as 800 pounds each. But that was nothing compared to how big George would get. At full growth, the Steller bull could take Alex's whole head easily into his jaws.

No, it would not be wise to bring George here.

It was too bad we couldn't build a gigantic display area especially for George, something wonderful with plenty of room for him and Ellie. But that would have cost millions of dollars, which we didn't have.

The thing many people don't realize about animal parks is that money is always very tight. No matter how much zoos or aquariums charge for tickets, it never seems to be enough. The main reason is the food that's fed to the animals. You can't feed an exotic animal junk and expect it to stay healthy. And high-quality food costs a lot of money.

Nobody got rich at Marine World. Divers started off at near minimum wage, and the salary never went up much, for anyone. Even Marine World owner Mike Demetrios had twice put up his own house for mortgage, borrowing money just to pay the bills. Clearly, we couldn't afford to build a special area for George.

We couldn't sell George to another zoo, either. Nobody wanted a huge, full-grown Steller bull to come rampaging into their lives. He ate a lot and was bad-tempered besides. We liked George, but then he was ours.

What were we supposed to do with him, as he grew and grew and grew?

Once, as part of the research I was doing for a magazine article, I asked if I could go into the pen with George to watch a trainer work with him up close, without any fence between us. Because I had been with the park for many years, and could be trusted to do what the trainer told me, I was allowed this privilege.

"Sure," said Bucko Turley. "Come on."

George was back in the pen at Seal Compound where his and Ellie's training had begun seven years before. Although he wasn't being trained for shows anymore, the trainers still tried to maintain a good relationship with George.

As we stood outside Seal Compound and Bucko fumbled with the lock, I felt my pulse accelerate. I had a pen and notebook in my hand. I would be taking notes, I thought.

To Bucko, sea lions were purely wonderful. He appreciated each individual's personality. I loved to watch Bucko with his animals — especially old Nero, who was getting on in years now. Sometimes when the two were together on the stage, relaxing in the sun, I imagined I could see

Bucko's face change just a little, his wrinkles and whiskers lining up differently, so he looked a bit like the sea lion beside him.

"I don't know what kind of mood George is in," said Bucko now, letting us into the main compound.

In the far pen, the Steller bull leaned on the six-foot fence, which bowed beneath his weight.

George was enormous; he now weighed roughly 1,500 pounds. His neck was as big as a giant man's chest, and his chest was vast. My knees went weak. I forgot all about taking notes.

The Steller turned his head and made a noise that I hoped was a greeting. I couldn't help noticing that his yellow-brown teeth looked bigger than my thumbs.

With another grunt the animal turned away. I knew logically that the ground did not shake when he sauntered off, headed in the direction of the white plastic target. But emotionally I felt I was looking into the cave of a prehistoric animal, something from another time and another world. I noticed that he didn't bother to actually touch his nose to the target as he was supposed to. He just stayed in that general neighborhood, and one big eye rolled back and looked at us.

"I think it's all right," said Bucko. "We can go in."

I followed, trying not to look as if I was hiding behind Bucko. I was not scared, I told myself. I was just nervous, and my stomach was a little shaky. Maybe I was coming down with the flu.

"We'll watch his whiskers," Bucko said. "When they fan forward, that's a sign of aggression." I watched his whiskers.

"It's too bad he's getting unhandleable," said Bucko as we approached. George shifted his weight and turned around.

"Seat up, George," said Bucko, indicating the training pedestal. George considered for a moment, and then obeyed, in no great hurry.

"Sonny had him trained so well there, for a while, like a regular sea lion," said Bucko. "But he's too big now."

Had the whiskers twitched a hair's breadth forward?

George breathed. His nostrils flared and then closed again.

"Okay, George, target," said Bucko. He stretched his arm in front of him. The massive sea lion leaned his head down and touched his closed mouth to Bucko's hand.

"Good boy, George." Bucko bent down to the large silver bucket at his feet. He had not brought the little red hip buckets trainers usually wore. They would not have held more than an appetizer for this giant.

"Watch his reflexes," Bucko said. He tossed a blue-skinned mackerel high in the air. As it fell I saw a blur, and then George had it in his mouth. But instead of eating the fish immediately, he tossed it, and caught it, and tossed it again. It looked playful, but . . .

"Come on, George, eat your food," said Bucko. George made another noise, and his eyeballs bulged. He breathed again, twice, and his whiskers rippled and then lay back.

Bucko's eyes stayed locked on George. I remembered something Sonny Allen had said. "A good trainer is not afraid, because he knows his animal. He's always watching for subtle cues, the signs of accumulating tension."

George swallowed the fish. Bucko handed him the next

one. George tossed this one, caught it, tossed it, and dropped it. But he did not bend to pick it up. "We're gonna have to cut this short," Bucko told me. Then he spoke again to George.

"No," said Bucko, and he was talking about more than the just-dropped fish. "No, George."

The whiskers flexed forward slowly, bristling out. The red-brown eyes were locked on Bucko. The eyeballs bulged until the white rings around them protruded from the sockets.

One flipper shuffled forward. George breathed again, twice more, rapidly, then held the last breath. The great head lowered on the enormous neck. His gigantic muscles hunched, George stepped down from the training pedestal, which put his bulk uncomfortably close to me.

"No, George."

Two wills were at war — that of the man, with his quiet intelligence, and that of George, with his mountainous strength.

Then the animal's gaze flickered and shifted. He wasn't afraid, obviously. But he looked beyond us, outside the pen, toward the little arm of the sea that ran behind the park. It was as if we had been dismissed, almost as if we were not there.

"Okay, George, in your house," said Bucko quietly. It was kind of funny, because we were already in George's "house." But Bucko moved and George responded, ga-lumphing along beside his trainer, as if they were playing a game.

They crossed the pen back toward the white plastic tar-get, and Bucko looked at me and then at the gate. I didn't run, of course. But neither did I need to be told twice what to do.

Bucko said good-bye to George and patted him firmly on the neck. George didn't seem to mind, but he didn't get excited, either. He was no puppy dog, eager to leap and fawn on a human. He was something of the wild, and so he would remain. We humans could not dominate him in any but the smallest ways.

As Bucko turned back to close the outer gate, I saw George leaning over his fence again, but he was not looking at us. He was facing outward, away from the park. The wind ruffled the gold hairs on his cinnamon coat; he breathed deeply, as if he smelled the sea.

9

Return to the Sea

On a gray March afternoon I saw George roaring in a storm. The rain was pouring down; individual droplets hit so hard they seemed to bounce on the puddles.

There was George, in the rain — head back, chest out. "AOURRRR! AOURRRR!" he roared, as if defying the lightning, daring the storm to come down and fight.

Dressed as I was in a wetsuit, rain was a source of pleasure to me. I sat down on a pile of old fencing to watch George, far enough back so he wouldn't think he had to charge the fence. A few days earlier George had scared the heck out of a bunch of rowdy kids who'd crowded too close to the pen, ignoring the sign that said STAY BACK FROM THE FENCE. George had done what was natural for him — he had charged the fence. The kids had moved back after that! But this far away, I didn't threaten George's peace, and he paid no attention to me.

He really was beautiful. The shades of his coat — red-brown, cinnamon, blond — combined in a multiplicity of patterns and hues. His mane, newly grown, was thick and full and shimmering gold.

He was almost fully grown now. The great physique was more perfectly streamlined than a submarine. He was a mass of muscle, smoothed by a layer of blubber under the skin that, while making him huge, gave no impression of fat.

Muscles fanned out across his huge chest. The big Steller's ivory-white whiskers were long and thick and straight as broom straws. His teeth were like a bear's; his red-brown eyes were large and unafraid.

He was so huge and strong, and yet there was some question whether George's species could survive on the same planet with humankind. With our sophisticated weapons and our careless treatment of the world's oceans, we could so easily wipe out George and all his kind. We had the power to just eliminate them from the face of the earth, as we have done to so many species before.

Humans haven't always been so destructive. As I sat watching George, I wished all people today could behave toward animals the way the Native Americans did. When Eskimo hunters killed a Steller like George, they thought a lot about it first. They even talked to the animal in their thoughts, thanking it for the gift of its life, which let their own families live. Talking to an animal in your thoughts might sound strange, but the professional animal handlers did it all the time. It focused their minds on the animal, so

that the animal became important. If something was important, you wouldn't waste it. The Eskimo hunters used
every portion of the animal they killed — hide, hair, and
flesh. Even the intestines of a bull Steller sea lion were used
to make a waterproof rain jacket flexible enough to fold up
in a pocket. The Eskimos and other Native Americans had
treasured the animals, and while they were in charge, America was a treasure house of wildlife.

But then came my ancestors, the Europeans. They came
from countries where game was relatively scarce, and hunting was closely regulated. Only royalty and the very rich
were allowed to hunt. Imagine how those people felt when
they got to America, and before them stretched a continent
full of animals. There seemed to be no end to the number
of creatures. Carrier pigeons were so plentiful that they
broke the limbs of trees with their weight. The good-tasting
birds were so fat and stupid that a child could kill one for
dinner with a stick. Out West, there were so many bison
that they were sometimes a hazard to railroad trains. The
conductors often stopped trains, passed out rifles to pas-
sengers, and let them shoot bison out the windows. Sometimes no use at all was made of the gigantic bodies. They
were just left to rot where they fell. The animals were killed
because they were in the way, or just for sport.

During the nineteenth century, Stellers, as well as other
pinnipeds such as fur seals, were slaughtered in huge num-
bers. In San Francisco, for example, people dining in a
restaurant called the Cliff House could once watch a beautiful Steller rookery on a nearby island called Seal Rock.
Today the Cliff House still stands, but Seal Rock is now
only a nervous resting place for a few scattered animals;

the original Steller rookery was slaughtered by local fishermen.

The Stellers were taken for several reasons. People from some Asian countries believed that drugs made from parts of Steller bulls' bodies would keep them strong and virile. They were willing to pay a lot of money for Stellers. Also, fishermen were convinced that Stellers and other sea lions threatened their livelihood by eating too many fish.

For example, in the commercial fishing area of Oregon's Klamath River, sea lions had been accused of eating all the salmon. Fishermen demanded that the game warden kill two big Steller sea lions that were thought to be eating the fish. The warden came and shot the two Stellers, and their stomachs were opened up. No salmon was found inside. But their bellies were full of lampreys. These vampirish, eel-like creatures have suction devices on their mouths that they use to prey on salmon. By eating the lampreys, the sea lions had actually been helping the fishermen.

Sea lions did take fish from fishermen's nets sometimes; there was no question about it. Of course, if the sea lions could talk, they would probably say that they were there first, and that the humans were netting millions of *their* fish! Besides, one scientific study done in British Columbia estimated the total damage sea lions did to the fishing industry, counting the fish they ate and equipment they wrecked (such as the nets they tore when tangled in them). Everything added up to 2.5 percent of the year's total ocean-fishing income. Two and a half percent is just a normal cost of doing business. Not only that, but the fish often followed the sea lions, so the sea lions actually meant *more* fish to the fishermen, not less. Nevertheless, the fishermen in British Columbia asked the government to kill the sea lions. Of a total population of 12,000 Stellers, 8,000 were killed.

Without the interference of humans, sea lions and fish once coexisted just fine. I had seen an old-time photograph of a big sea lion rookery right next door to a river mouth where the salmon came, year after year. Both animal communities were bustling with life.

The real problem today, I thought as I watched George, was that we humans were systematically overfishing the ocean. Then we blamed the sea lions for our own destruction of the fish population. Modern commercial fishermen were using vast nets, miles long, made of transparent fish line. The crisscross mesh was so small that the nets caught even young fish, which were killed before they could grow. Most horribly, the nets often broke apart in storms, and giant pieces floated away. These went on catching fish and strangling dolphins, seals, and sea lions, killing them without profit for anyone. These terrible nets were called "ghost nets" because of their near invisibility in water, and the fact that they killed and killed.

Worst of all, in addition to killing sea lions, human beings continued to dump our poisonous pollutants — oil, sewage, poisons from paper mills, and other industrial waste — into the ocean. The very waters in which Stellers and other sea creatures lived were becoming carriers of death.

And yet there was hope, too. All across the world, people were struggling to figure out where we had gone wrong. We were trying to understand what needed to be changed, and what needed to be left alone. We were learning how to clean up after ourselves, and how to become guardians of the earth instead of its destroyers.

All of this mattered to George very much, because he was being released to the sea.

Sonny Allen had recommended that both George and Ellie be returned to the ocean, in a place where they would have the best chance to survive. Park owner Mike Demetrios was in the business because he loved animals, and after thinking about it for a while, he said yes.

Inside his travel pen, George swayed excitedly, bobbing back and forth, shifting his weight, ready to fight if need be.

Something was about to happen. The day before, his trainers had fed him in his long, narrow travel pen. They had done this often before, throwing a bunch of his favorite herring to the back of the pen, so that he and Ellie had to go inside to get the fish. Then the pen door had been shut behind him and Ellie. This was how the trainers usually moved the big Stellers from one part of the park to another. Vets also used the small travel pen, or "squeeze box," when they needed to give George or another large animal a shot or an examination.

But now the travel pen was being used for a different reason. This time a heavy-duty forklift picked up the pen with George and Ellie inside. The machine set the pen on the back of a truck, much like the one that had taken them from the beach so long ago.

The truck took the animals down to the docks. George could smell and see the ocean. Then the travel pen was lifted and swung out over the water and onto a boat, the *Huck Finn II*, which would take the Stellers to the release location, off Año Nuevo, California.

The boat smelled of gasoline. As the waves lifted and dropped the boat, George's stomach felt very uneasy. Nauseated by the unaccustomed motion, he became frightened and was briefly seasick on the deck of the rocking boat. He backed up in the pen, almost squashing Ellie, until she bit him sharply.

After what seemed a long time, George saw the pen door open. The pen was at the very edge of the boat. The group of Marine World staff on board watched George and Ellie to see what they would do.

Below George was the ocean, green and unfamiliar, rising and falling. He looked down, and looked away.

Ellie crowded past. Without a backward glance she leaped, and a splash of white foam lifted as her body broke the water's surface. The people cheered and lifted plastic glasses of champagne in a salute.

George looked down at the sea again, while Ellie's head grew smaller in the distance.

There were no walls or fences ahead. Suspiciously George looked around and sniffed, but all he could see were the people on three sides of him, and the blue-green sea below. Two people stepped up close to him.

"Take 'er easy, big guy," said Bucko.

"Have a good life, George," said Sonny Allen.

George recognized the head trainer's voice and put his great nose on the white piece of plastic in the travel pen targeting for one last time, just in case the trainer wanted to give him a fish.

"Attaboy, George!" Sonny said with a half-laugh.

Then the giant sea lion took his nose away from the target forever. He shuffled forward and pushed himself out, toward the sea. George plunged through the air, fell, and cut the water with a lovely great splash. For a moment he seemed puzzled, and swam in a small circle, looking over his shoulder at the humans who had shaped his life for seven long years.

Then, with ease and grace and power, George took the direction Ellie had and disappeared into the ocean mist. The people cheered and took some pictures — of each other, the boat, the rocks, and the sea.

And then the people went away.

What happened to George after that? I don't know.

His future, like that of all his kind, is uncertain.

The national Marine Fisheries Service has just listed the Steller sea lion, *Eumetopias jubata,* as a threatened species. If something is not done to save the Stellers, one day their great roar may be heard no more above the surf, anywhere around the world. The Steller may vanish forever like another golden giant, the California grizzly bear, which once stalked the land in majesty but is now no more than a symbol on the California state flag.

Human-made dangers in the ocean — fishing nets, guns, timber wastes, and industrial pollution — are taking their toll. Steller researcher Dr. Robert Gisiner estimates that, in the past ten years, Alaska's population of Stellers has decreased by more than half. In other areas as well, the populations are seriously declining.

We humans are overfishing the sea, and poisoning it. We need to learn to control ourselves — to not take so many fish that we destroy whole species, to not pour the poisons

from paper mills and factories into the life-rich coastal shallows.

If we can protect the oceans instead of polluting them, then not only Stellers but all marine life will have a chance. The sea can be a rich source of life and wealth and beauty for all, for always.

There is reason to hope. All around the world, scientists and concerned citizens are joining together in the effort to protect marine life and the sea. Some scientists work with pinnipeds in general. Roger Gentry, Burney LeBoeuf, Ron Schusterman, Kathy Krieger, and others too numerous to name are devoting their lives to advancing people's understanding of the flipper-footed clan. For Stellers in particular, there is already a team of scientists, including Dr. Gisiner, that is preparing a long-range plan for that species' recovery. The scientists cannot do it alone, of course. What you and I as citizens do is perhaps even more important. There are only a few hundred pinniped scientists; but there are hundreds of millions of us. Every time we do even one small thing to protect the earth, even picking up the smallest piece of trash, we are fighting for the lives of all animals everywhere.

As for George and Ellie, they were young and strong when they were released to the ocean. They had a chance, though their lives would not be easy. They would have to catch their own fish and squid now; no one would bring them food any more. George in particular would have to fight hard — first in practice combat on the bachelor beach, and eventually against the real giants, the territorial bulls.

Ellie might well remain near Año Nuevo all her life. But

George, if he survived, might make the great migration of the Steller bulls. Guided by his internal compass, his body's natural awareness of the earth's magnetic pathways, George might head north, thousands of miles along the coast of North America, past California, Oregon, Washington, British Columbia — swimming on toward Alaska.

And if the storms were not too terrible, and he could dodge the nets and guns and killer whales, then one day George might see the shining peak of Mount Shishaldin up ahead. He would turn at the great sea pass of Unimak and make his way to the island of Saint George, where he was born.

Good-bye, George, and good luck — to you, and Ellie, and all your kind. May your roar be heard forever, wild lion of the sea.